C R E A T I V E   C R A F T S

MAKING
TEDDY BEARS

CREATIVE CRAFTS

MAKING TEDDY BEARS

Harald Nadolny and Yvonne Thalheim

STACKPOLE BOOKS

Contents

The football team 'Always on the ball', that is the motto of these five Girz bears from the seventies. These are the hopeful descendants of the famous Schuco teddies. These cheeky little chaps are 30 cm/11¾ in tall and a special feature is the wired body which makes them completely double-jointed.

Introducing the teddy bear

Everyone knows he can't hear, yet children have always told him their secrets. Everyone knows he can't speak, yet he has consoled many children.

No-one could claim that he is beautiful, and yet everyone is captivated by his charm. It's difficult to say exactly where this charm lies, for he can't see either ... though anyone who has looked a teddy bear in the face will have recognized the friendly twinkle in his knowing look.

For small children, my friend the bear is one of the best loved of all cuddly toys, and there can be no grown-up for whom he does not bring back childhood memories ...

The fact that collectors, too, have discovered the 'colourful world' of the teddy bear was clearly revealed when old teddy bears began to fetch sensational prices in British auctions.

With this book on my friend, the teddy, I would like to take you back to the time of the early 'bear age'. I will introduce you to some of the veterans who are still around and tell you about the teddy's past in a short historical section on page 7. This includes a glance at how a fierce foe turned furry friend.

You will also find everything you need to know about making your own bear. There are full instructions and cutting patterns for each of the teddies included in the book.

Choose yourself a 'bear friend'. There is something for everyone, ranging from simple, small mascot bears to beautiful, fully movable, professional teddies. And, of course, the teddy's close relatives, the panda and the polar bear, have not been forgotten.

On behalf of my friend I would like to wish you pleasure in reading this book and in making a 'dream teddy'.

My friend A bear of the younger generation studying 'bear history'.

Collecting teddy bears

History of the teddy bear

There is an old Russian proverb which says: 'Feed the bear in winter and he will not eat you in summer'. And in the days when Bruin still prowled freely through European woods, the sight of one of his paw-prints was enough to turn our forefathers' blood to water. For centuries his enormous strength and size made the great brown bear one of man's most feared enemies. Despite, or because of, the threat he posed the bear has always held a fascination for man. Cave-men long ago made his image in clay and drew hunting scenes of bear fights on their walls.

The Indians of Arizona worshipped a bear god, which they sought to appease with wild dances. Bears' claws worn around the neck were said to give the wearer the strength of the mighty beast. It was for the same reason that the bear became a popular heraldic symbol in Europe alongside the lion and the eagle.

The bear also plays an important part in many old tales and legends. Here he often appears as the powerful protector of a princess, or he finds and rears a human baby that later becomes a great hero. In the fairy tale of Snow White and Rose Red a bear becomes the friend and playmate of the two beautiful sisters.

Long before he developed into the furry-eared 'teddy', the friend and playmate of countless children, lovable bears – standing on their hind legs – featured in advertising. They were used to sell baby foods, sweets and fizzy drinks. There was even a company which advertised its pianos with a series of drawings of dancing bears.

It is generally accepted that the 'history' of the fabric bear began in the early years of this century, around 1902/3, though as early as the mid-nineteenth century there were, in Germany, papier-mâché bears covered in fur, on four wheels and with a ring through their noses. These were realistic representations of the dancing bears which were taken from village to village as circus attractions. Another nineteenth-century manufacturer of toy bears, Nicolas Schanne, was to be found in Paris. In 1887 his son wrote a book about his father's toy factory.

These were the first Steiff's four-legged bear on wheels recalls the fierce creature of real life. He is the forerunner of the fabric bear sitting beside him.

This bear in his trousers and crocheted jumper has everything you could wish for in a beautiful old teddy: shoe-button eyes, long curved arms and a prominent nose. Both bears date from 1910.

The telephone call Two generations of bears are brought together: Minky Zotty, the brown baby teddy of 1969, is soft, round and furry; the gold-coloured grandad teddy of 1903 looks much more like his real-life counterpart.

Bed-time whispers Bears can adapt to the most varied surroundings and particularly enjoy luxury as we can see from Petsy (1928) and Zotty (1952).

The battle of the bears

Experts and teddy-lovers alike still argue about the events surrounding the manufacture of toy bears in the early years of the twentieth century, although the achievements of the Steiff toy factory in Germany and the Ideal Toy Corporation in America are generally recognized. It is agreed, however, that the name 'Teddy' has something to do with President Theodore Roosevelt (1858–1919). One popular version of the story, current in the American press between 1902 and 1905, originated from the pen of Clifford Berrymans, a well-known cartoonist. He drew the President refusing to kill a young bear captured during a hunting expedition. Numerous versions of the story were in circulation, but we know that Berrymans invented the incident. Nevertheless the cartoon caused quite a stir and led Morris Michtom, who owned a stationery and novelty shop, to display two toy bears in his store. His wife Rose had made them herself – from light-coloured fur fabric, stuffed with wood wool and with two black shoe buttons for eyes. Apparently Morris Michtom asked Roosevelt if he could use the shortened version of his Christian name and call his new fabric toy 'Teddy's bear' and Teddy Roosevelt agreed.

These toy bears were a great success. Michtom set up a bear factory which was to become the largest in America, the Ideal Toy Corporation.

At the same time a further episode in 'bear history' was being enacted in Germany. To be precise, the bear boom was starting in a small village in Württemberg. Margarete Steiff (1847–1909), who was confined to a wheelchair by polio, earned her living as a seamstress. In her spare time she also made little elephants from spare bits of felt which she stuffed and gave to the children of the neighbourhood as toys. The elephants were so popular that other larger animals followed: a donkey, a horse and a pig, until eventually, by the turn of the century, the whole family was involved in the business.

Her nephew, Fritz Steiff, who was an art student, persuaded his aunt to make a fabric bear based on drawings he had made at Stuttgart zoo. This new creation was first shown at the Leipzig fair in 1903, but aroused little interest. Just before the fair closed a representative of the New York company F.A.O. Schwarz appeared and ordered 3,000 bears on the spot. Margarete was overwhelmed by the size of the order. Practically everyone in the village had to help to complete it on time. In 1903 the Steiff company made a total of 12,000 bears. By 1907 its output had risen to 974,000. Soon the Steiff company was known as the Giengen 'Bear Factory' and took a bear's head as its trade mark. Another trade mark that came later was the familiar metal tag in the bear's ear.

Steiff too have their own version of how the fabric bear came to be called 'Teddy'. Early Steiff bears were used as table decorations at the wedding reception of President Roosevelt's daughter. Teddy Roosevelt was so enchanted with the bears that when he was asked what sort of bears they were, he replied: 'Teddies, of course'.

The American magazine 'Play things' which had included news of the little furry fellow from his beginnings in 1903, first used the term 'Teddy bear' in 1906. Up till then the fabric bears had been referred to as 'Bruin', 'Friend Bruin' or simply 'Brown bear'.

The virtuoso Petsy, a Steiff bear of 1928, is in excellent condition. It is clear that no child has ever played with him.

Old bear with shoe-button eyes His matted fur has developed a few bald patches, but he is still loved by old and young alike.

9

The French bear His pointed nose and red paws give him away although his beautiful condition hides the fact that he is a grandad teddy dating from 1920.

The British are coming Chad Valley and Merrythought bears are known far beyond the shores of Britain.

Bear psychology

It is said that nothing can stop an idea whose time has come, and time was ripe for the teddy bear. The teddy bear fulfils a basic human need that is as clear and simple as the need to eat and drink. Konrad Lorenz, for example, saw the teddy bear as evidence that people need something to take care of. Children's doctors in Britain and America usually have at least one of these furry friends in their surgeries because their ability to reassure and console sick children is unrivalled. Even autistic children, who reject all human contact, will warm to their friendly gaze and begin to play with them.

But early in 'furry bear history' a number of warning voices were raised. The Church was especially worried, fearing a drop in the birth-rate for, as the clergy said: 'A little girl playing with a bear does not pretend it is her baby as she does with a doll.' A great curse was seen to be spreading throughout America with the teddy bear, the curse of racial suicide! But on the other hand it was said it did not matter whether maternal or paternal love was awakened by a doll or a bear, for it was still love. Authors such as Claire Henning, who seriously concerned themselves with this problem, recognized another important factor ... the teddy bear provided boys with a toy they could love without being told: 'Little boys don't play with dolls.'

The bear boom

As it became clear that the teddy bear was to be a permanent feature of the toy market, some manufacturers began producing all kinds of accessories to go with him, as well as trying to design other products that could cash in on his success. Soon after the introduction of the teddy there appeared on the American market a host of 'teddy products', bear postcards, for example, bear books and teddy bear plates and cups for children's parties.

For the fabric bear himself there was a complete collection of specially designed clothing which, of course, had to be kept in specially designed drawers and wardrobes. As well as the familiar growl, he learned to sing and to make quite lengthy speeches. He began to walk and could perform simple gymnastic exercises. There was even a teddy doll – a bear with a doll's face on one side of the head and a teddy's face on the other – and a curious double-sided teddy with a doll's head at one end and a teddy's head at the other.

There were no limits to the possibilities, which explains why nowadays we ask: 'What makes a real teddy?'

Collectors know exactly what the answer is. For them a real teddy bear must be made of mohair (hair of the Tibetan goat). It must be able to stand upright, which means it must be two-footed, and it must have fully movable arms and legs and a revolving head. A really good teddy bear will also have a hump back and a long nose. Both are signs of age and character. A teddy's value is increased if it has a pleasant facial expression. Real collectors also look their bears straight in the eyes.

There is a practical reason for this testing stare; you can tell from the shape whether the eyes are modern plastic or the good old glass. It is sometimes possible to tell the manufacturer from the eyes' colour.

The list of what makes a teddy could go on and on. It both sounds and is confusing. The only way someone beginning collecting can get 'an eye for a bear' is to look at as many teddies as he can, noting the differences between them and the distinguishing features of each (see the table on page 26). The teddy collection on the following pages can provide only a limited view of the many types, species and classes of the great kingdom of the teddy bear.

Paddington Every British child is familiar with him. According to the children's book about him, he arrived at Paddington Station in London from 'darkest Peru'. He had nothing in his suitcase except an almost-empty jar of marmalade and wore a label round his neck which read: 'Please take care of this bear. Thank you!'.

11

Teddy bears from 1900 to 1929

The American bear *(top photo)* This 60 cm/ 2 ft teddy is a so-called Michtom bear of the Ideal Toy Corporation of America. A typical feature is the shape of the muzzle. The bear has gold-coloured mohair fur in good condition and is fully movable.

The playmate *(bottom photo)* Old 35 cm/ 1 ft 2 in Steiff bear in good condition, with movable arms and legs and revolving head. It has a pronounced hump and still has the original Steiff tag in its ear.

The good life *(large photo right)* This 47 cm/ 1 ft 6½ in Steiff bear has golden mohair fur, movable arms and legs and revolving head, large feet and long, curved arms.

Patient Patience *(top photo)* Gold-coloured bear with shoe-button eyes, movable arms and legs and ears on the sides of the head.

Tired bear *(bottom photo)* Light-coloured Schuco bear is fully movable. The embroidered nose and mouth are typical, but the shoe-button eyes are unusual in Schuco bears.

The morning wash *(large photo right)* Beautiful bear with a lot of character from 1903. He has gold-coloured mohair fur and measures 60 cm/2 ft.

Teddy bears from 1930 to 1949

Baby-sitter wanted *(top photo)* Two of Steiff's sought-after baby teddies. They were made in 1930 and each measures only 25 cm/10 in. Unlike other bears, their fore-paws face downwards rather than inwards.

The Asian bear *(bottom photo)* An early example of a panda, this one is a Steiff panda of 1938. He has movable arms and legs.

Aunt Emma *(large photo right)* 'Unused' Steiff bear of 1930, measures 35 cm/1 ft 2 in, has gold-coloured mohair fur and the original ear-tab.

More tea? Made in white mohair, the baby teddies are much sought-after. The 26 cm/10½ in standing bear is by Steiff; the seated teddy is by Hermann and measures 22 cm/8½ in. The open mouth is characteristic of both.

Music at home These three Steiff bears are really quite musical: the piano-player squeaks when he is squeezed, the teddy on the piano growls and the bear with the brown trousers plays '*Guten Abend, gute Nacht*' thanks to a Swiss musical box concealed in his tummy.

The two friends Both bears are fully movable. A striking feature of the teddy on the right is his white glass eyes. His fur is in excellent condition.

The polar bear The brown bear was not the only one that was loved as a faithful friend, with his fluffy fur the polar bear also won the hearts of many children.

Hungry bear *(top photo)* Ruf bear in good condition, with black velvet patches on paws. He too has a tag in his ear – in the right ear this time.

When grandfather plays with the train *(bottom photo)* You can certainly tell that they have passed through the hands of numerous children, and yet these two bears, both measuring 65 cm/2 ft 2 in, are in excellent condition. In the truck is a Schuco bear (1960).

Teddy bears from 1950 to 1970

Brothers together *(photo right)* Two fully movable grizzly bears. Note the open mouth of the large long-haired teddy.

Pair of pandas *(bottom photo)* These rare Hermann bears with revolving heads are extremely well-made and of outstanding quality. Holes in the paws of the large panda show that it was originally on wheels.

Hand of cards *(large photo right)* Both bears are fully movable and of extremely high quality. The small teddy is by Steiff, the large one by Hermann. One distinguishing feature is the reddish eye colour of the Hermann teddy.

The gambler This Steiff bear with its movable arms and legs and revolving head measures only 15 cm/6 in and is rarely found in this colour.

Always on the move This 18 cm/7 in bear starts moving as soon as his scooter is wound up. The inscription on the metal scooter: 'U.S.-Zone-Germany' shows that it was made soon after the war.

The do-it-yourself bear *(photo right)* Rare 'Yes and No Bear' from Schuco – moving the tail makes the head shake or nod. This 30.5 cm/1 ft bear has a fabric body with only the head and paws in mohair. He is cutting out a circle for a bear's joints.

First day at school *(photo top left, page 22)* These two little fellows are both by Steiff. The brown bear with the label and ear-tag is a rare example from the early fifties.

Bear family *(photo far left, page 22)* Mother and baby come from the Berg factory in Austria. This manufacturer makes bears with particularly sweet faces. The red heart is the trade mark of Berg bears. Next to them sits a Hermann Zotty. Typical of the Zotty generation is the open mouth and long hair.

The bear's family tree

When an old teddy bear came under the hammer at Sotheby's of London for around £6,000/$3,900, it caused a sensation. The news spread like wildfire through the international media. Completely unnoticed by the general public, this children's favourite with its matted fur had become an object of great value, worth as much as an antique item like an eighteenth-century English writing-desk. And the teddy was still not 100 years old. The first fabric bears did not appear until the beginning of this century, their official date of birth being 1903. Since then there have been so many different makers and so many different types that identifying a teddy has become quite a science. But with a little practice you will soon be able to distinguish an old veteran from a more recent addition to the bear family.

The earliest bears have triangular-shaped heads, long curved arms down to their knees, long feet and a long muzzle. The heads of modern bears, on the other hand, are round and the arms and feet have become shorter. The whole effect is softer. Old bears are long and thin with a prominent hump and have unstuffed ears on the side of the head. It is interesting to note how the ears have moved continually upwards in the course of time. Teddies of the first generation often have a seam along the middle of the head, running between the ears to the tip of the muzzle. Another typical feature is the black shoe-button eyes. Glass eyes on pins did not come until later. Since many children swallowed the bear's eyes, only unbreakable glass or plastic eyes, securely attached to the teddy's head, are used nowadays. The stuffing has also changed. Straw and wood wool have been replaced by modern, fire-resistant fibres fulfilling strict safety requirements. One sign of an old bear is the extremely solidly stuffed stomach of the veterans. Straw and wood wool were not the only fillings used in the early bears. Some were filled with kapok, cotton wool, cork, and even sawdust or shredded paper. It was only from the mid-sixties that manufacturers began to use synthetic fibres. Recent advances in fur fabric have not been for the better, for the dralon fur used since the sixties does not compare with the pure wool mohair fur of the early days.

To become a real expert on teddy bears you will need to familiarize yourself with the distinguishing features of different manufacturers. The first stage is to recognize labels. Each firm has its own emblem, but these have tended to change in the course of time. The Steiff company had two trade marks, firstly the small label on the bear's neck and secondly the tag in the left ear. The inscription on the label has changed four times since the firm was established, while the shape of the tags has changed five times.

Diagram 1

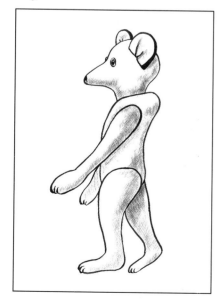

Diagram 2

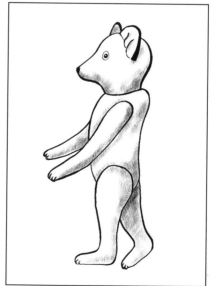

Diagram 3

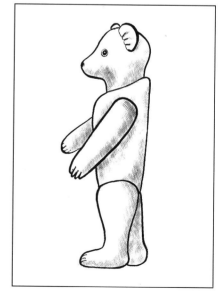

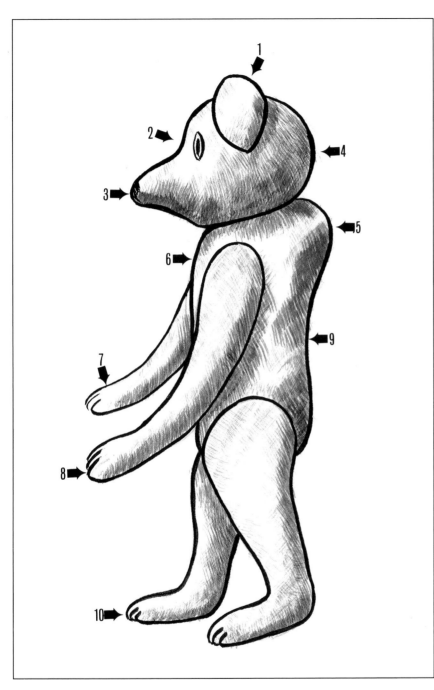

Diagram 4

Since distinguishing marks like these can easily be lost, you will need to be able to recognize other typical characteristics. For example, Schuco bears usually have quite a fierce expression, arising from the company's style of embroidering the mouth and nose. The firms of Hermann and Steiff can also be distinguished by the nose, although they are more easily recognized by the embroidered claws, Steiff bears always having four and Hermann bears three. Steiff eyes are light brown whereas Hermann eyes shine with a reddish light. If you come across a bear with particularly short feet, it may well be a Clemens bear. If your unrecognized favourite has especially long arms you could find it is a Petz teddy. And so the list goes on . . .

For the sake of completeness, it should be said that even 'unmistakable' features can lead you astray. Odd examples of button-shoe eyes existed right up to the late forties while a few firms were making short, straight arms as early as the thirties. Many irregularities in the manufacture of teddy bears were due to the war, when firms changed their usual style to use whatever materials they could get hold of. There will be some bears that even the experienced collector is unable to recognize, but he will certainly be able to distinguish between the genuine article and a fake.

Distinguishing features of old bears

1. Unstuffed ears placed on the side of the head
2. Flat glass or shoe-button eyes
3. Long pointed nose
4. Triangular head
5. Prominent hump
6. Mohair fur
7. Long curved arms
8. Felt pads on paws
9. Wood wool or straw filling
10. Long legs with large feet

Teddy bear features

	ARMS	LEGS	BODY	EYES	HEAD	SPECIAL FEATURES
1903–1920	long curved arms almost to knees 3 or 4 claws felt patches	long legs large feet 3 or 4 claws felt patches leather patches	large hump growl wood wool or straw stuffing solidly packed	shoe-button or glass eyes very flat	ears on side of head triangular head, poss. with centre seam unstuffed ears	long pointed nose good mohair fur
1920–1930	long curved arms ½ body-length 3 or 4 claws felt patches	long legs medium feet felt patches 3 or 4 claws	medium hump growl solidly packed	glass eyes very flat	ears on side of head	
1930–1950	curved arms ½ body length felt patches 3 or 4 claws	long legs medium feet felt patches 3 or 4 claws	growl small hump solidly packed	glass eyes flat	higher ears	
from 1950	slightly curved short arms felt or synthetic patches	short legs small feet felt or synthetic patches	soft synthetic filling	glass and plastic eyes flat	ears on top of head rounded head	synthetic fur no hump
Steiff	4 claws very good felt patches curved arms	4 claws very good felt patches	very good mohair	brown		tag in left ear
Schuco	slightly shorter arms	3 and 4 claws		sometimes metal eyes light brown	large ears pointed nose slightly fierce expression	often mechanical "yes-no"
Hermann	3 claws	3 claws	good mohair	red	friendly expression	embroidered nose outer stitches pulled down
Clemens	3 claws straight arms usually fabric patches	3 claws usually fabric patches		reddish-yellow		small stunted feet
Petz	3 claws very long arms	3 claws		reddish	long nose	porcelain tag on chest
Grizzly	3 claws	3 claws			round face	often Zotty-type long fur

Bear hunting

Teddy bears are everywhere, but when you are specially looking for one they all seem to disappear! Just like someone gathering mushrooms, a bear-lover must become familiar with the habitats and habits of his favourite species before he can hope to find them.

The favourite habitats of old teddies are lost property offices, junk shops and antique shops. But they have also been spotted at jumble sales, auctions and flea markets. Remember when you are visiting doll exhibitions or antique or toy fairs it is the early bird that catches the worm. The best bear will probably be sold in the first few minutes after opening. That does not necessarily mean that the best is irretrievably lost. It is not unknown for the same bear to be sold a few hours later at the same fair, but at a third of the price again.

The same thing applies to flea markets, which are becoming more and more popular. Here you can make a good catch, especially in summer when more private individuals hire stalls, since the professional dealer trade tends to return in the autumn.

You might also find a good old teddy by advertising, but the days are unfortunately gone when you could exchange a new toy for an old teddy. Since the teddy hit the headlines, his popularity has set prices rocketing. If you build up your collection on the American lines of 'learning by going'

Steiff jubilee bear
Unfortunately it is possible to forge a teddy bear. Remember that manufacturers bring out reproduction bears to mark special occasions which can fall into the wrong hands and be trimmed to look like an old bear.

or, as we would say 'learning by your mistakes', you will find it a very expensive procedure.

You can learn a lot about the appearance and distinguishing features of old teddy bears from illustrations in old magazines or books, but you can learn even more from an experienced collector. Contact with others who share your interest not only helps you gain a good eye for a bear, but also keeps you up to date with current prices. You may be lucky enough to come across someone you can trust who knows about bears and will help you when you start. For, in addition to the jungle of ages, types and classes, there are a number of other factors which affect the value of a teddy.

Dark brown or white fur is, for example, particularly sought-after, while grey is the least popular colour. Golden yellow and beige fabrics do not affect the price providing the fur is in good condition, 'never played with' as bear collectors say. If the teddy still has the original label or tag, this increases the price by around 15–25 per cent. Badly damaged bears, on the other hand, may lose as much as 50 per cent of their value. It does not usually matter if the paw patches are damaged, for collectors will not usually worry if the paws are slightly frayed. Replacement eyes are also quite common and do not affect the value so long as genuine old eyes have been used. Shoe-button or glass-pin eyes were often lost or removed by cautious parents for safety reasons. A replacement arm or leg, on the other hand, can bring down the value of a teddy by as much as a third. The same is true if the bear has lost his growl or if a mechanical bear no longer works.

In the table
Anyone involved with fabric bears for any length of time will know that no two teddies are the same, and it is only with experience that you can learn to distinguish the special characteristics of the separate groups of bears.

27

This all sounds very clear cut, almost as if all you need when you buy a teddy is a tape measure, but all the criteria we have mentioned so far count for nothing if the teddy has 'that certain something'. Since no two bears, particularly no two old bears, are the same, in the final analysis it is the personal taste of the buyer that determines what he will pay for his new furry friend.

If all the early Steiff bears on the market today were genuine, Steiff would have had to double their actual output. The crudest way of faking a Steiff bear, and also the most difficult to detect, is by embroidering the famous four claws on to a similar bear. Next comes the label swindle. It requires more dishonesty than skill to staple a famous trade mark to an anonymous bear. Bitter experience has taught collectors to look behind the eyes because if a teddy has been bleached it will not penetrate behind them and the fur will still be the original colour. It is just as easy to tell the difference between glass and plastic eyes, for plastic eyes have sharp corners at the outside edge.

Occasionally the big manufacturers bring out reproductions of their early bears. It is not hard for an unscrupulous forger to trim the fur and to resell them as old bears at an inflated price.

Ultimately you may only be able to tell if your expensive teddy bear is really 50 or so years old by cutting open his tummy: old wood wool is brown while the more modern version is pale beige.

Naturally everyone would like to be told the precise value of old teddies but, as in other areas, the price depends on supply and demand. Since the Americans tend to be even keener 'bear hunters' than the Europeans and many bears are exported to America, much will depend on the dollar rate, just as it does in the stock market. If the dollar rate is good, prices will be high.

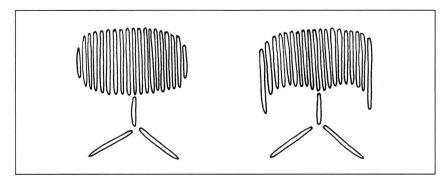

Steiff and Hermann bears are often very similar in quality and design. One way of telling the difference is by the nose: Hermann noses have a longer stitch at each end which is lacking in the Steiff noses.

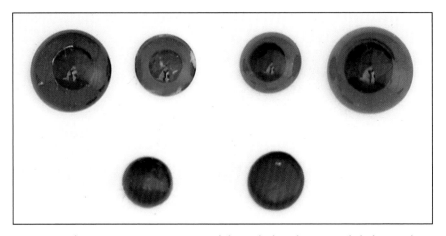

Gazing into a bear's eyes can sometimes reveal the truth about his origins: light brown glass eyes are used by Steiff, reddish glass eyes by Hermann, while black eyes are the sought-after shoe-button eyes.

Naturally an old bear should be stuffed with old wood wool which is darker in colour than the modern version. Unfortunately, you will have to cut your bear open to find out what he contains.

Visitors from the North Pole Two Steiff bears, made around 1950. The blue eyes are typical of the four-footed polar bears.

Bear glove puppet This also dates from the fifties and was made by Steiff.

This makes it impossible to give any precise figures, for within a month the situation might well change. This means that while a teddy may occasionally fetch over the £6,000/ $3,900 quoted, whether a teddy's price could rise much higher than that is another matter.

But who are we to say that it is only old bears that are worth collecting? Most pre-1940 bears are already in private collections and new bears have the added interest of being much more difficult to identify. Basically any teddy that is well made and with his own individual charm has a good chance of increasing in value. The bears on sale today offer a wide choice of collectors' items for the future. This is especially true of the limited editions from known makers who produce unique teddies by hand.

Many collectors prefer to specialize. You could try building up a collection of particularly small or particularly large bears or concentrating on one particular manufacturer. Popular makes include Berg (Austria), Felpa (Switzerland), Merrythought (England), Skine (France) and Lenci (Italy). Käthe Kruse of Germany is another maker of beautiful bears. In addition there are a host of other teddy products which you could collect; postcards with bear pictures, for example, teddy books, pendants or brooches, porcelain bears or cutlery with teddy motif handles.

The bear family has also grown in recent times. A teddy glove puppet or bear muff are just as much part of it now as the panda or koala and even face flannel bears have joined the family. But you should not be surprised when you occasionally come across a humble, brightly coloured bear with synthetic fur and, possibly, movable limbs and head for sale at a give-away price and your collector friend tells you: 'That's not a teddy bear.' What you see is a fairground bear which collectors have not yet accepted into the family.

Restoring teddy bears

Caring for your bear

Regardless of whether your teddy is a toy, a mascot or a collector's item, he can bring you lifelong happiness. If you follow a few basic rules, he will continue to look as good as new.

Caring for a new fabric bear is extremely easy. If he spends most of his time sitting on a shelf all he will need is the occasional light going over with a hand vacuum cleaner, but if he is your child's constant companion and playmate he will need washing several times a year. Now and again you will also need to repair minor damage such as split seams or small holes. None of this is difficult, nor is it expensive in terms of time or materials.

Things are different, however, when a veteran teddy comes to live with you. He will usually have more wrong with him than a mere split seam. If he has a leg hanging off, an eye missing or badly worn paws he will require a fairly major operation.

You need to be much more careful when cleaning an old teddy than the quick wash given to a new one. Old bears are usually stuffed with straw or wood wool and you should avoid getting them wet. The external fabric will also have become weak and may rip unless it is handled very gently. After paper, fabrics are the most difficult materials to maintain. Ultraviolet light, for example, is a great enemy of old teddies, so do not stand them in direct sunlight or fluorescent light. The old gent's sunbathing days are over. Another enemy is water vapour. Keep your bear away from coffee makers, egg poachers and anything else that produces steam. Kitchens or damp cellars are not the places to keep an old bear.

You should also protect your old teddy from fluctuations in temperature and excessive dust. Impurities in the air will not only make him dirty but will also eat away his fur. Worse still are flour mites, silverfish or even woodworm. In the space of six months these unwelcome parasites can leave your wonderful long-haired Zotty bear totally naked of fur. So, although the idea of quarantine is often regarded as something of a joke, you should take it seriously and put it into practice.

Just as an animal entering a new country has to be kept under observation for a while, a teddy bear should be kept in isolation before he is allowed to join the other bears in your collection. A suitable place to keep him is in the freezer. This is no joke — most collectors of teddy bears have an old freezer in the cellar to deal with new additions and emergencies.

The new teddy should be sealed in a bag and kept in the freezer for at least a week. Then he should be shaken and brushed in the open air. In order to get rid of the most resistant parasites, the teddy should be thoroughly sprayed with an anti-vermin spray and again sealed in a bag. After 48 hours the bear will come out of the bag as clean as the day he was born.

Much-used Steiff bear from the first series. If this bear could only talk his story would fill a book.

The doctor's visit It doesn't usually take much to put a bear back on his feet. The three little Steiff bears are very well cared for, and will obviously need only a routine examination.

Cleaning

Here again we have to differentiate between old and new teddy bears. Some new bears can even go in the washing machine, but do not try it unless it is specifically recommended in the washing instructions. Put the teddy in a pillow case and wash him at the recommended temperature.

Any bear which can be machine-washed will usually be all right in the tumble drier. Here again protect him by putting him in with a sheet or bath towel and choose the fine fabric setting.

If you want your teddy to be really soft and fluffy, brush up his fur when he is dry with a soft nail brush.

Even when you hand-wash your teddy, you must make sure that the body contains nothing that could be damaged by water, such as a growl mechanism, straw filling or cardboard joints. After his wash you should lay your teddy on a large towel and, if possible, dry him in the open air. A good brushing will bring up his fur beautifully.

An old bear cannot withstand being immersed in water and should certainly never be machine-washed. They require special handling and should be dry-cleaned.

With a colour-fast carpet cleaner you can clean the bear's fur without damaging the stuffing. Rub plenty of bubbles into the fur using a damp brush, leave to dry for 24 hours and then carefully go over him with a vacuum cleaner.

The oldest and safest way of cleaning a teddy bear is to wash the fur with soap-suds. Place the bear on a large,

Prevention is better than cure Bears need to be looked after properly and, as we see, these four baby teddies are enjoying the soap bubbles.

clean towel (if he has pin-mounted glass eyes these should be removed first). Make some mild soap-suds by adding liquid soap to a small basin of warm water. Brush the suds on to the fur with a soft washing-up brush, shaking excess water off the brush to avoid wetting the filling. Work the bubbles into the fur with a light, circular motion. Avoid brushing seams and the felt pads on the paws as you could damage them. Finally wipe off the suds one area at a time with a damp dish-cloth. Place the clean teddy on a dry towel and dry gently with a hair-dryer, combing the fur with a wide-toothed metal comb. The more tousled the fur, the coarser the comb. A metal dog comb is ideal. Your teddy will look really good if you finish the fur with a fine-toothed 'de-lousing' comb.

The glass eyes can be cleaned quickly with liquid ammonia before being put back in place.

Dealing with minor injuries

There are two different circumstances in which you will have to help a bear back on his feet. In the first, it is repairing a child's favourite playmate. Here any repairs can be carried out to suit the personal taste of the owner of the bear, making sure they are strong enough to withstand any future rough handling. The second is a case of carefully restoring a teddy to its original condition in order to increase its value. Here careful handling is required. Everything must match down to the smallest detail. This means that you cannot give a twenties' teddy blue plastic eyes, for it would have been made originally with the sought-after black shoe-button eyes. To help with repairs most collectors have a 'teddy drawer' in which they keep old bears' eyes in various sizes and colours as well as old voice mechanisms, labels and tags.

You can find these special items on old soft toys. Experienced collectors will search flea markets, auctions and jumble sales for old soft toys which are damaged beyond repair. You can even use the fabric from an old toy, since new fabric used to patch up an old bear would be too noticeable. Another way of getting hold of spare parts is to write to the manufacturer. With luck they will send you the original item you need by return of post.

Step 1

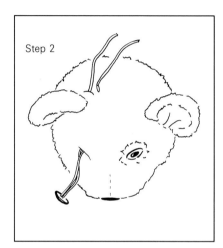

Step 2

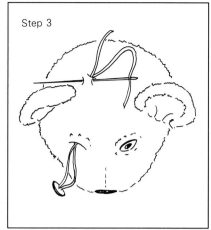

Step 3

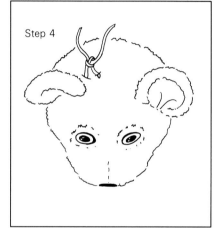

Step 4

A missing eye

If you have to replace a missing eye, you can choose between pin or wire-mounted glass or plastic eyes and black semi-spherical button eyes. If you cannot find the perfect match, you will have to replace both eyes, in which case all you have to do is to make sure that the new eyes are more or less the same size as the old ones.

To attach the eyes you should use a strong thread. Place the thread through the ring on the back of the eye and thread both ends through a long darning or upholstery needle. Push the needle into the fabric, taking care to place it precisely where you want the eye to go (step 1), through the filling in the head and out again behind the ear (step 2).

Make sure that the eyes are level. Take one end of the thread back into the fabric and bring the needle out about half a centimetre from the other end (step 3). Pull both ends tight and tie them in a knot as close as possible to the head. Cut off the ends of the threads and conceal the knot in the fur (step 4).

Renewing paw patches

On most bears the paw patches are made of felt. They can range in colour from pale beige to dark brown. You may find difficulty with matching patches of a specific colour in old makes of bears. Here you can dye the felt with tea, but this is a job that calls for a lot of patience and practice. Normally when replacing paw patches you use scraps from an old felt hat or an old felt lining.

Cut a piece of felt, making it about 1 cm/⅜ in larger all round, of the correct shape for the patch. Carefully cut away the worn patch with scissors and place the new piece of felt over the hole in the paw. Use a crochet hook to push the excess under the fur, so that the new felt patch is positioned in exactly the same place as the one you have taken off. Sew it into place with small overcast stitches and comb the fur over the join.

Split seams and small holes

A teddy that hasn't got at least one tear is not a real teddy! The bottoms of the arms and the shoulders are usually the first to go and you should examine them carefully before washing the bear. A split seam may look quite serious as the stuffing will usually be spilling out, but is in fact very easy to repair. Push the stuffing back into the bear using the blunt end of a crochet hook. Using a thread to match the colour of the fur, close the seam with neat stitches (top diagram), keeping as close as possible to the edge of the fabric.

If the teddy has a hole and the fabric around the hole is worn, you will have to draw the edges together with ladder stitch (lower diagram). Make the stitches around 15 mm/⅝ in from the edge of the fabric and turn the frayed edges in using the blunt end of a crochet hook as you sew.

Replacing an ear

Replacing an ear is not as bad as an eye operation. It can be performed even by those with the most delicate stomachs. Pin the loose ear to the bear's head and sew it on with small stitches.

If you want to sew it on really firmly you can also run a row of stitches along the back of the ear. It is a different matter entirely, however, if one ear is missing. You should remove the remaining ear from the head and separate the two halves. Then cut two pieces the same shape as the front of the ear in felt. Use these for the front of the ear and the original fur pieces for the back. This means that each ear will now consist of a felt front and a fur back. Complete ears and sew both to the bear.

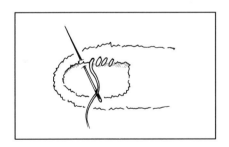

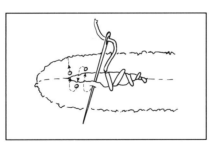

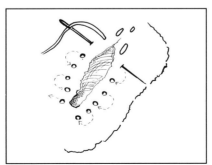

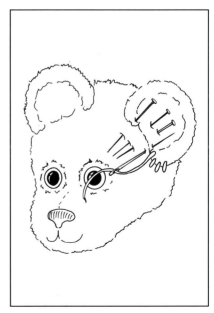

Restoration

Most people still have an old teddy tucked away in a trunk or gathering dust in the cellar or attic, but not all of them will look as dilapidated as the poor old teddy in the following illustrations.

At the beginning of the twentieth century he was a dashing young bear, with movable arms and legs, soft felt paws, dark eyes and wonderful golden-yellow fur. More than 60 years later he is a mere shadow of his former self. The felt patches have been replaced several times and his stomach has been repaired with thick yellow thread. The eyes are missing (step 1). In this condition the teddy is worth almost nothing.

While he does not look brand new after restoration, he has the inimitable charm of the old teddy bear, a charm possessed by no new fabric bear, no matter how expensive. In addition our teddy has risen in value and would now fetch a decent price on the open teddy market.

Our teddy after the total operation. You can see how good he feels.

Step 1

36

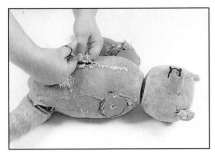

Step 2

Step 3

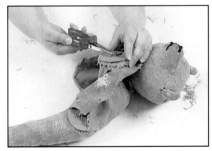

Step 4

Step 5

First the poor old bear's tummy is opened up. The thread holding the two halves together is thick, so nail scissors are used to cut through it (step 2). For finer threads you should use a seam opener. First the top layer of stitches is cut, then the underneath layer. Take care not to damage the fabric itself. Any remaining bits of thread are pulled out with tweezers.

The wood wool is pulled out by hand. This is quite a dusty job. The brown colour of the wood wool shows that the teddy is quite early. New wood wool is light beige in colour (step 3).

Removing cotter-pins

It is clear that the discs which allow the limbs to move are still in good condition, so the cotter-pins are straightened out with round-ended pliers (step 4).

The discs are carefully removed.

Keep all the bits, however small, for you may not always be able to find matching cotter-pins in your 'teddy drawer'. Any seams or mends that have not been properly sewn or were done with poorly matching thread must be removed. This will inevitably produce holes (steps 5/6).

Making good arms and legs

Any 'new' threads should be removed from the paws as well as any replacement felt patches. Once again make sure that you do not damage the fur fabric itself (steps 7/8).

Getting a soft toy ready

To patch any holes in the bear's fur you can use an old soft toy. Treat it in the same way as the bear's body, cutting open the seams and removing the stuffing (step 9).

Step 6

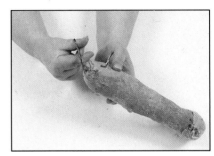

Step 7

Step 8

Step 9

37

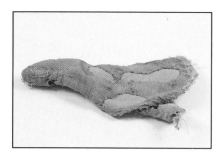
Step 10

Step 11

Step 12

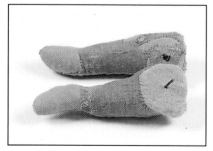
Step 13

Patching a hole

Make good the hole by trimming away any frayed fabric. Place a suitable piece of the patching fabric under the hole and pin it into place. Turn a little of the old fabric under and sew with overcast stitches (step 10).

Restuffing arms and legs

Once you have patched all the holes in an arm or leg, except for the hole where the paw patch is to go, it can be restuffed. Always start by stuffing from the bottom up. Tease the wood wool apart and distribute it as evenly as possible (step 11).

Replacing paw patches

If you need to replace the paw patch, start by removing the old felt. Trim the edges of the fur fabric. Place the felt on the paw and cut around the shape of the paw, allowing a 1 cm/$\frac{3}{8}$ in seam. Push the felt under the fur fabric in the same position as the original patch. Sew into place with overcast stitches (step 12).

Inserting discs

Place a cardboard disc and washer together and push the cotter-pin through them. Place the disc under the fabric of the inner arm or leg and push the pin through the hole. Make sure there is no wood wool between the disc and the fabric. Finally sew up the opening (step 13).

Step 14

Step 15

Replacing eyes

If you have to replace the eyes, use wire-mounted eyes as with these you can be sure of getting two eyes that match exactly. First cut the wire to a 2 cm/$\frac{3}{4}$ in length using wire cutters and then, using round-headed pliers, bend the wire to form a ring. Thread a strong, unbreakable thread through the ring and thread both ends through a large darning or upholstery needle. Push the needle in exactly where the eye is to go and bring it out again at the centre back of the head. Repeat with the other eye, making sure that the eyes are level. Pull the threads through firmly and knot them as close to the head as possible (steps 14/15).

Step 16

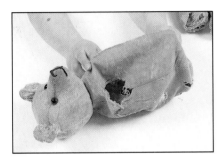
Step 17

Step 18

Step 19

Replacing ears correctly

Ears are the most likely part of the teddy to be damaged and on our bear they have been torn off several times in the past. The old ears should be removed and made good, replaced in the existing holes on the head, pinned and sewn into place with small stitches. Make sure you sew the ears on really tightly because they are often used to pick up the bear.

Restuffing head

To restuff the head start by carefully opening up the chin seam. Insert your fingers and compress the existing wood wool into the head. Add as much new wood wool as you need and resew the seam (step 16).

Lining the body

Use the lining method described for the limbs to patch any holes in the bear's body. This not only repairs any damage but also strengthens the weak fabric so that it can eventually be firmly stuffed (step 17).

Rejoining arms and legs

Push the cotter-pin at the top of one leg into the matching hole at the base of the body. Slide a cardboard disc and washer on to the end of the pin.

Using round-headed pliers curl each end of the pin under on to the disc (steps 18/19).

Repeat with the other leg and the arms.

Stuffing the body

Finally stuff the body. If you are using new wood wool cut it into short lengths before use. Then sew up the tummy (steps 20/21).

Step 20

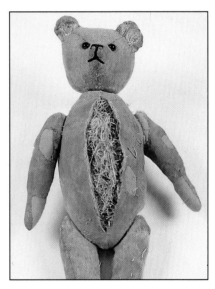
Step 21

Making teddy bears

Bear selection

Now is the time for you to choose from the engaging bear assembly presented in this chapter. The bears are laid out in their separate anatomical parts from page 70–79, just waiting for you to bring them together to form the perfect teddy.

First of all, everything you need to know about completing the exercise successfully is detailed – from fabric, fillings and movable parts to giving your bear a growl and a pair of winning eyes.

Here is the cast of teddy bear personalities from which you'll then be ready to select a favourite:

Naturally, patterns for a suitable wardrobe are provided too, on pages 66–69.

The bears introduce themselves
You can make all the hard-working bears we see here and learn all you need to know on the following pages.

The whole thing usually begins quite innocently. You want something nice to give to your small nephew or niece or to a grandson or granddaughter for a birthday or Christmas present. What could be better than a cuddly teddy bear that you have made yourself?

You will know from your own experience how much pleasure a soft toy like this can give. Despite computers and video games things have not changed much.

All the teddies included here can be made at home, and they are easier and quicker to make than you may think.

Once you have decided to make a teddy bear, the first thing you have to do is to buy the fur fabric and stuffing. Then arms, legs, head and body are cut out and sewn together. Once the first baby bear has been born, its maker will have fallen undyingly in love with her work. You may not believe it, but you will find it's true. In most cases it is impossible to give away that first teddy. It is the second one that becomes the gift.

The matter does not rest there. As soon as word gets around that someone in the family has such an unusual talent, there will suddenly seem to be twice as many children in the family, all wanting a teddy just like the one you made for your godchild or grandchild.

But that is impossible. No two home-made bears ever turn out exactly the same, even though you use the same pattern and follow the instructions precisely. The new bear will have a personality of his own which makes him different from all his brothers. On the other hand, you can use the same pattern to create bears which are entirely different. By using a fabric with a different length of fur you can turn a slim little fellow into a well-fed chubby little chap. The difference will be even more striking if you change the colour of the fur or size of the bear.

It is precisely the fact that you cannot predict exactly how things will turn out that is the great attraction in making teddy bears, added to the fact that making them is easier than people think.

The sections are easy to cut and can be sewn by hand or with a sewing machine and the stuffing shouldn't cause any problems either.

The only thing you really have to concern yourself with is choosing the right materials. Teddy bears look best when they are made in a fabric that is as close as possible to real fur.

When choosing the eyes it is worth spending time to find ones that have the right expression and which are the right size. Glass eyes give the face of a fabric bear more life than other types, but even black semi-spherical eyes will give the teddy its familiar 'trusting look'. There is also a difference between a bear made as a toy for a small child and one as a mascot for an adult.

All you need to know is explained in the following pages. And you will soon see how true it is that teddies seldom come singly . . .

Cutting

The secret of good sewing lies in precise cutting. This begins with tracing the patterns. The more carefully the sections are copied and cut, the easier they will be to sew together later. Since the fabric used for teddy bears slips easily and is quite thick, it is a good idea to make cardboard templates. To do this trace the patterns in this book on to greaseproof paper and, using carbon paper, transfer them on to cardboard. It is important to copy all symbols, like the arrows showing the direction of the weave and lines for darts. Mark each section to show what piece it is (arm, leg, body), what fabric it is in (fur, felt) and how many you need to cut. Later when you have cut them out you can keep identical pieces together by threading them on to a piece of cotton or keeping them in an envelope.

If you want to enlarge a pattern or make it smaller, mark a sheet of paper with 2×2 cm/$\frac{3}{4} \times \frac{3}{4}$ in squares and place it over the pattern. Square off another piece of paper with larger or smaller squares and copy the pattern square by square.

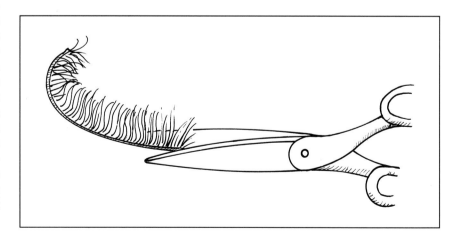

Fabric

As we have already said, the fabric for the teddy should be as close as possible to natural fur. Suitable fabrics include imitation fur, fur fabric, teddy fabric, plush and velvet. If you cannot find what you are looking for in a handicraft shop, you may find the fabric department of a large store or even a furniture shop can help. When buying fabric make sure you get a woven rather than a knitted fabric. Woven fabrics are firm enough to keep their shape when stuffed. To achieve the same firmness with a knitted fabric you will have to iron a backing on to it.

Before cutting, establish the weave of the fabric (which way the threads run) and stroke the fur to find which way it lies. All the sections to be cut in fur fabric are marked with an arrow showing the direction of the weave. When positioning the patterns on the back of the fabric the arrow must follow the weave. Make sure, if you mark the fabric with tailor's chalk, that all the markings on the pattern piece are copied on to the fabric. Cut out the sections adding the recommended seam allowance. It is best to use small, extremely sharp scissors. Always cut the fabric backing, never the fur (see diagram left).

For any section where you need two or more, place the pattern the other way up on the fabric and cut out again.

It will make your work easier if you run a line of tacking stitches along any of the markings that will eventually disappear inside the teddy, for example, points where arms, legs or eyes will be attached.

Since velvet and fur fabrics slip easily when sewing through a double layer of material, it is a good idea to pin and baste the seams before sewing. When you are using a long-haired fur fabric, the hair may get caught in the seams and should be pulled out again with the point of a needle.

Fillings

The final appearance of your teddy bear depends to a large extent on the material used for the filling.

Dacron and polyester is the most commonly used filling because it is easy to work with, does not form lumps and is completely washable. You can get it from hobby and handicraft shops.

Many old teddies are stuffed with **wood wool**. This is lighter than most other fillings and so is ideal for large bears. It should not be allowed to get wet, however, or it goes out of shape. Wood wool is easier to work with if it is first cut into smaller pieces with an old pair of scissors. You can get wood wool free of charge from china shops or other places where it is used as packing material.

Kapok is another non-washable filling. With kapok you can stuff your bear and then mould it into shape from the outside. Even the smallest paws can be stuffed perfectly with this material. Kapok is heavy and so is not recommended for large bears. It is available from drapery shops.

Untreated sheep's wool is a wonderful filling material, but is unfortunately difficult to get hold of. It is washable and you will not need much of it for each bear.

Foam chips are inexpensive and readily available. They are fully washable. Remember, all soft toys must be kept away from fire and foam chips should be avoided altogether in teddies for tots. Foam chips should only be used to stuff smaller bears. Never use them for solid teddies that have to be modelled, nor for those with movable arms and legs. When using this material it is a good idea to work on a large sheet of polythene or paper. Cut up larger chips with scissors before use.

TIP:
Check all seams before you begin filling. Start by filling the least accessible places such as arms, legs and head. Make sure you stuff right into the tip of the muzzle. Never take too much filling at a time to avoid lumps and air holes. The teddy should be nice and firm and smooth all over. To push the filling into arms and legs, use the handle of a wooden spoon. When stuffing larger bears, left-over bits of fur fabric can be cut up and used as part of the filling for the body.

Eyes

Glass eyes give a teddy the most lively expression. They are available in two styles (each in different sizes) from hobby and handicraft shops. The eyes are sold singly with a ring on the back (like a button) or in pairs (joined by a wire). The wire is cut before use and bent with pliers into a ring (step 1). The technique of attaching the eyes is identical for both. For this you need very strong thread, preferably binding thread, and an upholstery needle (available from specialist sewing shops).

Once the bear's head is stuffed all it needs are the eyes and ears. Push the needle from the point where the ear will go at an angle through the top of the head, bringing it out just above the muzzle (step 2). Thread an eye on to the thread and take the needle back to where the ear will go (step 3). Pull the thread tight and tie in a knot. When you sew on the ear it will cover the thread (step 4).

In many cases black shoe-button eyes will suit the teddy better. They are attached in exactly the same way as the glass eyes.

If the teddy is intended as a toy for a small child, it is safer to embroider the eyes. Alternatively you can cut small circles of felt, a small black one for the pupil, a slightly larger one for the iris and a larger one still for the white of the eye. The felt circles should be sewn together before attaching them to the head.

Safer than glass eyes are the machine-washable acrylic eyes with a stalk and metal washer. They are attached to the head before it is stuffed. Press the stalk through the fur fabric from the right side and press the metal washer on to it. This anchors the eye firmly to the fabric.

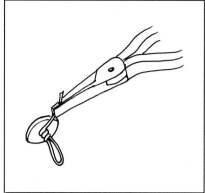

Step 1

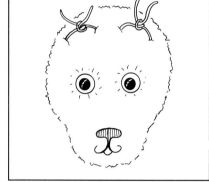

Step 3

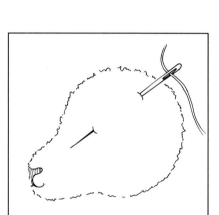

Step 2

Step 4

The movable joints Left to right: plastic, cardboard and plywood discs. Also shown are cotter-pins and the washers used with them.

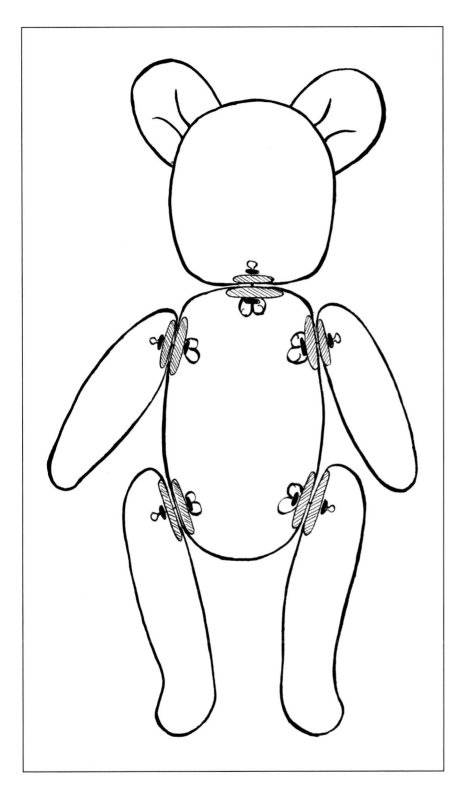

This is how the 'joints' look in the completed bear.

Voice

It is extremely easy to give your teddy a growl. All you have to do is to remember to put in the voice mechanism when you stuff the body. You can, of course, always put a voice into an existing teddy. To do this you will have to unpick part of the front or back seam, take out a little stuffing, insert the voice mechanism and sew up the seam again.

Discs

The discs are the teddy's 'joints'. It is these that make his arms and legs move and his head turn. The size of the discs depends on the diameter of the neck and the top of the legs and arms. Plastic discs in various sizes are available from handicraft shops. If the bear is to be stuffed with a non-washable material, you can make your own discs to the size you need from thin plywood. For each joint you will need two discs, two washers and a cotter-pin.

Making a teddy with movable limbs

If the teddy is to be played with it is a good idea to give it movable limbs. To attach the arms, first stuff the arm and sew it up leaving the seam at the top of the arm open. Thread a washer and then a plywood disc on to a cotter-pin. Push the pin through the fur at the top of the arm at the point where it is to be attached to the body. Then sew up the seam at the top of the arm. Before stuffing the body push the pin through the appropriate point on the outside of the body and place a plywood disc and a washer over it. Using pliers, roll the ends of the cotter-pin under. Make sure the ends are tightly rolled or the arm will become loose with use.

Embroidering the nose and mouth

Either thick, black wool or shiny, black embroidery silk are ideal for embroidering the nose and mouth. The size of the nose and mouth depends on the size of the teddy bear. Begin at the tip of the nose. You can make a knot in the end of the thread as this will eventually be covered by the embroidery. Fill in the triangle of the nose with a series of closely placed stitches and finish it off neatly by taking a few stitches across the top of the nose.

The mouth is an inverted 'Y' joined to the tip of the nose. You may find you have to do several stitches on top of one another to make it show up through the thick fur.

You can also buy plastic bear noses in various sizes, and if you use one of these you will only have to embroider the mouth. Alternatively you could cut a nose from leather or felt and stitch it to the bear.

Before you start it is a good idea to have a look at a few bears to get a feel for the shape, size and positioning of the mouth and nose, for these are the features that will give your bear its character.

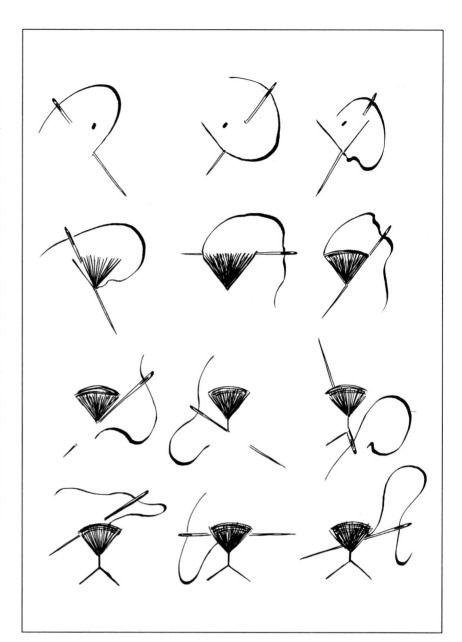

Embroidering the claws

With the same thread you used for the mouth and nose, you can also embroider the bear's claws. The knot at the end of the thread will be hidden by the fur.
Important: Never embroider more than four claws! (diagram 1).

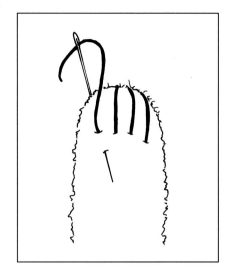

Sewing stitches

The best stitch for sewing fur fabric is blanket stitch. This is sewn on the right side of the fabric. Blanket stitch gives an almost invisible seam which makes it particularly good for sewing together the different furry sections of your bear (diagram 2).

Scallop stitch is used mainly to prevent cut edges from fraying. When making your bear it can be used to sew the paw patches into place. The compact row of stitches gives a neater look than overcast stitch (diagram 3).

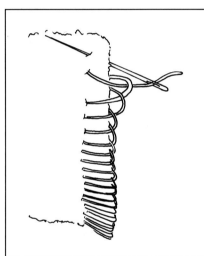

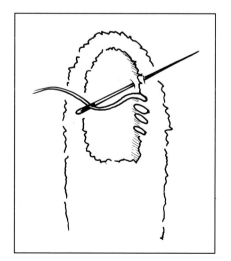

A teddy for a baby

There are two things you should remember when making a bear for a small child: it must be completely safe, so that the child cannot injure himself on it, and it must be completely washable.

Children can be injured by glass eyes which they pull out and swallow. The same applies to plastic noses. You can avoid any danger by embroidering both the eyes and nose. Teddies with limbs that move by means of cotter-pins and discs are again unsuitable for babies. It is better to sew the arms and legs into a fixed position. Large teddy bears are unsuitable for small children, who can easily trip downstairs when clutching a big bear.

If a teddy is to be washed frequently you should use a synthetic fur fabric or possibly a wool mixture.

For the filling use washable dacron and polyester, which retains it shape extremely well. Unfortunately there is no voice mechanism that will withstand the washing machine.

48

Bear species

Quick and easy bear

The next time you are invited out, how about surprising your hostess with an unusual thank-you gift? She will always be able to find room for a teddy like this. And if you make it small enough it could go on a key-ring.

Making up
Cut out two body sections, allowing an extra 0.5 cm/¼ in for the seam. From the felt cut one each of the paws and

Materials
0.4 m/⅜ yd brown woven fur fabric (1.4 m/54 in wide)
light-coloured felt (remnant)
black darning wool
2 glass eyes
dacron and polyester filling
The cutting patterns can be found on pages 70/71.
The bear is about 22 cm/8½ in long.

muzzle with no seam allowance. The two body sections are sewn with right

sides together. Leave an opening on the inside leg to allow you to turn the body the right way out and for stuffing. Snip through the seam allowance at all corners and along curves. Turn the body the right way out, stuff the bear and sew up the seam using blanket stitch. The felt patches are sewn to the arms and legs using scallop stitch. Sew on the muzzle using an overcast stitch, stuffing it with a little filling. Embroider the nose and mouth using black darning wool. Finally insert the eyes, following the directions given on page 60.

Bill and Ben

Wherever these two little rascals make their home, there will always be some mischief afoot. Any child would be delighted with them. If you buy teddy fur in a knitted fabric, you will have to iron a backing on to it before cutting to help the teddy keep its shape when stuffed.

Materials

0.3 m/$\frac{1}{4}$ yd brown fur fabric
  (1.4 m/54 in wide)
dark brown fur fabric (remnant)
red felt for the tongue
dacron and polyester filling
1 bear's nose, 2 glass eyes
1 upholstery needle, scissors, pins
dressmaker's chalk
all-purpose glue
The cutting patterns can be found
  on pages 70/71.
The bears are around 40 cm/
  1 ft 4 in tall.

Making up

Except for the red felt tongues, all sections should be cut with a 1 cm/$\frac{3}{8}$ in seam allowance. Two paws, two foot-pads and two ears are cut from the dark fur fabric. All other sections are in the light fur fabric.

Check the lie of the fur before cutting and make sure you transfer all the markings from the pattern pieces.

Fold each leg section right side together and pin the centre seam, placing the pins at right-angles to the edge and pushing the fur to the inside. Sew up the centre seam. Pin and sew the footpads to the bottom of the legs so that the guide numbers coincide. Turn the legs the right way out.

Sew the paws on to the arm sections. Fold each arm section right side together and sew up the side seam. Turn the arms the right way out.

To make the head, start by placing a light and dark ear section right sides together, and sew along the rounded outer edge. Repeat for the other ear. Then turn the ears the right way out and sew into place on the front side sections of the head. With right sides together, baste the centre gusset of the head into place between the two side sections (with the ears inside). Baste the centre seam of the sections for the back of the head. With right sides together, baste the back of the head to the front along the side seams. Machine all the seams, making sure you catch the ears in the stitching. Sew the centre seam of the muzzle. Sew the muzzle into the round opening at the front of the head. Put in the dart on the edge of the neck. Turn the head the right way out and stuff it.

Sew the centre seam of both back and front sections. Lastly sew the side, inside leg and shoulder seams. Insert the arms and legs into the appropriate openings, sew, and turn the body the right way out. Stuff the legs, body and arms with dacron and polyester filling. Using a strong thread hand-sew the head to the body. (You may find you have to gather the neck slightly to make it fit.) Insert the eyes, glue on the nose and sew on the red tongue.

To make the bib you will need a scrap of cotton, preferably with a small pattern. You will find the cutting pattern on pages 68/69.

Cut two bib sections, each with a 1 cm/$\frac{3}{8}$ in seam allowance. Sew the two sections right side together, then turn the right side out and run a line of quilting stitches 0.5 cm/$\frac{1}{4}$ in from the outside edge.

Make a buttonhole in the top left corner and sew on a button top right. Alternatively the bib can be secured with a press-stud.

Bear family

Whether you decide to make John, the stern-looking father bear, or Josephine, the friendly mother bear, or whether you decide on one of the baby bears, all are made from the same basic pattern. All are fully movable and stuffed with wood wool. The parent bears are 52 cm/1¾ ft in height and the babies 26 cm/10 in.

Materials

0.5 m/½ yd brown fur fabric
   (1.4 m/54 in wide)
about 20 × 20 cm/7¾ × 7¾ in felt
wood wool
2 glass eyes
10 thin plywood discs (8–10 cm/
   3¼–4 in diameter)
5 washers
5 cotter-pins
button or other strong thread
black embroidery silk
1 upholstery needle
scissors, pins
dressmaker's chalk
1 pair pliers
The cutting patterns can be
   found on pages 72/73, 74/75.

Place all your materials ready

Making up

Copy the patterns from the book on to cutting-out or brown paper. Lay the patterns out, lining up the arrows with the direction of the weave, on the wrong side of the fur fabric. Hold them in place with large basting stitches to prevent them slipping during cutting (step 1).

Cut out each section (without seam allowance). Then cut the paws from felt. Transfer all the markings from the patterns to the fabric. Mark the points where the eyes, arms and legs are to go with a line of stitches (step 2). Place the outside and inside leg sections right sides together and pin in position, placing the pins at right-angles to the edge and pushing the fur inside. Oversew edges with zig-zag or overlock stitch (a sewing machine stitch specially for stretchy fabrics). Leave a section of seam open for turning, and leave the legs open at the bottom for the footpads (step 3).

Sew the footpads into the bottom of the legs, lining up the two number 9s (step 4).

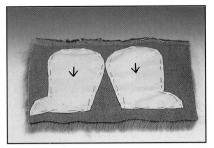

Step 1

Step 2

Step 3

Step 4

Step 5

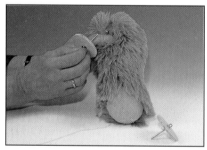

Step 6

Step 7

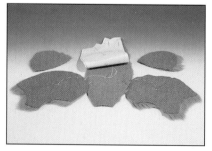

Step 8

Sew the felt paws on to the inside arm sections and sew the outside and inside arm sections together. Leave an opening for turning. Turn all the limbs the right way out and stuff with wood wool (step 5).

Sew up the openings with blanket stitch (step 6) unless the teddy is to have movable arms and legs. For these insert the 'joints' before you sew up the opening. First thread a washer and a plywood disc on to the cotter-pin and place it into the opening with the point projecting outwards. Make sure that they match exactly on arms and legs (step 7). The head is made from six separate sections (step 8).

Begin by sewing the sides to the centre section. Lining up the numbers, sew the muzzle into the head. Then, with one seam, sew along the centre of the muzzle and down the neck (step 9).

Turn the head the right way out and stuff. To make the ears, sew two ear sections together, leaving them open where they join the head. Turn the ears the right way out and sew on to the head using blanket stitch (step 10).

Place a disc and cotter-pin in the opening at the neck and gather up the edge of the neck opening with button thread. Knot the ends firmly and fasten off (step 11).

Embroider the nose and mouth with black embroidery silk; see page 46 (step 12).

Using an upholstery needle and black button thread, attach the eyes, as shown on page 60 (step 13).

Step 14 shows the sections completed so far. All that is missing is the body. Place the body sections right sides together and sew the centre front and back seams, leaving an opening for turning. Sew up the side seams and turn the body the right way out.

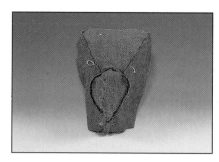

Step 9

Step 10

Step 11

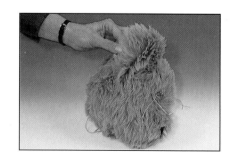

Step 12

Step 13

Place the stem of the cotter-pin which is sticking out of the head into the top of the body where the four seams meet. Place a plywood disc on to the pin and with pliers roll under the two stems of the pin firmly (step 15). Fix the movable arms and legs to the body in the same way. Finally stuff the body. The bear will stand nice and upright if you compact the stuffing well in the lower half of the body (step 16). Sew up the back seam with blanket stitch. Use a needle to tease out the fur along the seams and give the fur a comb if necessary.

Step 14

Step 15

Step 16

Who wouldn't like to have this bear for his own?

Clothes for the bear family

Accessories like garden furniture, dummies and spectacles can be bought in toy shops. The bear family's clothes are quick and easy to make.

For the dress you will need:

Materials
about 0.5 m/$\frac{1}{2}$ yd small-patterned cotton
0.5 m/$\frac{1}{2}$ yd narrow white lace
1 press-stud
Cutting pattern is on pages 66/67.

Fold the fabric double. Adding a 1 cm/$\frac{3}{8}$ in seam allowance all round, cut one each of the front of the dress and front yoke along the fold of the fabric. Cut 2 each of the back of the dress and back yoke. Sew the shoulder seams of the yoke. Neaten the neck edge with bias binding. Make a narrow hem round the bottom and up the back edges of the yoke. Sew a strip of lace on to the bottom of the yoke. Make a narrow hem around the front and back arm holes and sew up the side seams. Sew up the centre back seam to the opening. Make a narrow hem along each side of the opening. Run two rows of stitches around the neck edge and gather it to fit the yoke. Baste, then sew to the neck. Make a lace bow and sew it to the front of the yoke. Hem the dress and sew a press-stud to the back of the neck.

For the jacket you will need:

Materials
0.5 m/$\frac{1}{2}$ yd fine dark-brown corduroy
fine light-brown corduroy (remnant), 6 small buttons
Cutting pattern is on pages 66/67.

Lay the pattern pieces out on the fabric and cut out, allowing 1 cm/$\frac{3}{8}$ in for seams. Use the light corduroy for the collar and revers and dark corduroy for all other sections. Sew the shoulder seams together. Make a 0.5 cm/$\frac{1}{4}$ in hem at the bottom of the sleeves. Sew in the sleeves. Sew up the side and sleeve seams in one continuous row of stitching. Sew the collar sections right sides together and turn the right way out. Sew one open edge of the collar to the outside of the neck opening. Neaten the neck opening by turning under the other open edge and sewing to the inside of the neck. Line the lapels and front opening with the revers. Top stitch around the collar, lapels and front opening close to the edge. Make the buttonholes on the left front and sew the buttons to the right front.

For the dungarees you will need:

Materials
jersey towelling remnant
elastic
scraps of fabric for appliqué hearts (optional)
Cutting pattern is on pages 66/67.

Place the towelling double and cut out the dungarees without seam allowance. Hem the bottom of the legs, the bib and arm holes. Sew up the side and inside leg seams. Then run elastic round the bottoms of the legs and along the front and back of the bib. Cut narrow strips from fabric and sew to the bib as straps. You might like to add some small appliqué hearts.

Polar bear

It is bitterly cold where the polar bear lives amongst the ice floes and pack ice of the Arctic circle. Our bear, however, prefers human habitations where he can satisfy his insatiable desire to be cuddled. In return he will tell the best bedtime stories this side of the Arctic circle.

Materials
0.5 m/½ yd white teddy fur
    (1.4 m/54 in wide)
about 20 × 20 cm/7¾ × 7¾ in light
    brown felt
dacron and polyester filling
2 blue glass eyes
1 long darning needle
scissors, pins, black embroidery silk
dressmaker's chalk
The cutting patterns can be found
    on pages 78/79
The bear is about 15 cm/6 in tall.

Making up
Cut all the sections except the footpads from the white fur with no seam allowance. Make sure the arrows are lined up with the weave and transfer all markings from the pattern to the fabric.

Pin each outer body section to an inner section, right sides together, and join the side seams, oversewing the edges with zig-zag stitch. Fit the felt footpads into the bottom of the legs so that the numbers line up.

Insert the head gusset as indicated between the two body sections. Sew the back seam and the back part of the tummy seam.

Close up the centre muzzle seam. Join the muzzle to the body, sew the neck seam and continue in one line of stitching along the front of the tummy seam.

Stuff the bear with dacron and polyester filling, and then sew up the

opening in the tummy seam by hand, tucking any excess material into small pleats.

Place the ear sections right sides together and sew round the curved edge. Turn the ears the right way out and sew to the head, in the position indicated, with blanket stitch.

Fold the tail along the dotted lines, sew edges together and then sew on to the bear.

Embroider the nose and mouth with black embroidery silk. Last of all attach the eyes following the directions given on page 34.

Teddy bear gang

Children can't help but fall in love with these cheerful chaps and fortunately these bears with their plastic disc joints and brass cotter-pins are well prepared for all the attention they will receive. It will not matter if Siggi, Taps, Mona, Karlo (*from left to right*) and Sunny (*standing*) get dirty during their romps. Placed in a pillow case they can be machine-washed at 30°C/86°F, for they have a synthetic filling.

Materials

0.38 m/$\frac{3}{8}$ yd light brown mohair fur (0.75 m/29 in wide)

about 20 × 20 cm/$7\frac{3}{4}$ × $7\frac{3}{4}$ in dark brown felt

about 200 g/7 oz dacron and polyester filling

2 glass eyes with rings

4 plastic discs with centre hole (1.8 cm/$\frac{3}{4}$ in diameter)

6 plastic discs with centre hole (4 cm/$1\frac{1}{2}$ in diameter)

5 metal washers (brass)
5 cotter-pins (brass)
sewing thread
dark brown wool
1 long darning needle
scissors
dressmaker's chalk
buttonhole silk
flat-headed pliers, pins
The cutting patterns can be found on pages 74/75.

The cutting patterns can be found on pages 74/75.

Step 1

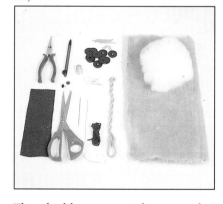

The double paw patches are also designed to withstand rough treatment. Since these smart little fellows are bound to be extremely popular, we have included instructions for two different sizes. Bears made to the basic pattern are 32 cm/$12\frac{1}{2}$ in; bears from the smaller pattern, 22 cm/$8\frac{1}{2}$ in tall.

Step 2

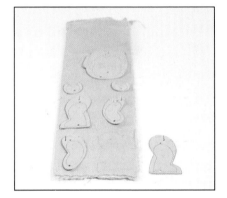

Step 3

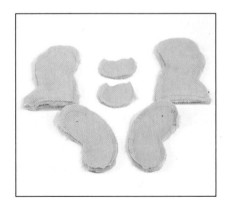

Step 4

Making up

Get out all your materials before you start. The job will be much easier if everything is to hand (step 1).

Check which way the fur lies and fold the fabric in half, right sides together, in line with the lie of the fur. Since fur slips easily, pin and baste along the edges (step 2).

Lay the following seven pattern sections on the fabric: two leg sections, two arm sections, two ear sections and one side body section. Make sure the arrows are lined up with the lie of the fur. Using dressmaker's chalk draw round the patterns on to the fabric. Make sure that you transfer all the markings (step 3).

Baste each section along the marked lines and then machine sew, making sure you leave openings where marked. On the side body sections also leave the shoulder seams and darts open. Cut out the pieces, allowing 1 cm/$\frac{3}{8}$ in for seams. Only at the ear opening should you cut directly along the line. Neaten the cut edges with zig-zag stitch (step 4).

Copy the markings for the darts and the number for the leg and arm holes on to the wrong side of the body sections. Put in the darts, cut them and flatten out. Sew up the shoulder seams at right angles to the front tummy seam, making sure that point 1 is in line with point 1 – this will mean gathering the front seam slightly (step 5). Again allowing 1 cm/$\frac{3}{8}$ in for seams, cut two side head sections (1 reversed) and one centre head section (step 6).

Pin the head sections together so that points 2, 3 and 4 coincide exactly. Baste the seams. When you eventually sew them you will have to gather the centre section since it is slightly larger. Sew the back neck seam (step 7).

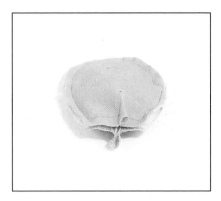

Step 5

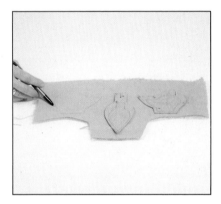

Step 6

Step 7

59

Step 8

Step 9

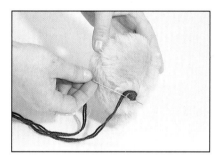

Step 10

Step 11

Flatten out the seams at the nose, push out the nose and mark the point where all the seams meet with a needle. Pin, baste and sew the chin seam. Turn the head the right way out (step 8).

Begin by stuffing the top of the head with the dacron and polyester filling. Then stuff the back of the head until flat (step 9).

Embroider the nose with dark brown wool. Take the needle up through the neck opening and bring it out at the tip of the nose. Use three to four stitches to make the nose. With the last stitch bring the needle out once more at the tip of the nose and embroider the inverted 'Y' of the mouth. Bring the thread back through the head and knot the two ends (step 10).

The eyes should be sewn with strong thread. For these bears, push the needle into the back of the head and bring it out where the eye is to go. Place an eye on the thread and bring the needle out again at the back of the head. Leave the threads hanging for the time being (step 11).

Turn the ears the right way out and pin them loosely to the head. By drawing up the threads from the eyes and moving the ears you can change the teddy's expression until you find one you like. Then fold the ears slightly and sew them into position with blanket stitch. Knot the threads holding the eyes firmly together at the back of the head (step 12).

To insert the joint for the head, first place a washer over the cotter-pin and then a 4 cm/$1\frac{1}{2}$ in plastic disc. Place the disc in the neck opening with the pin pointing downwards (step 13).

Baste with strong thread and gather in the neck opening, then sew firmly into place around the pin (step 14).

Adding a 1 cm/$\frac{3}{8}$ in seam allowance, cut two footpads from dark brown felt and two from light brown fur. Place a felt and fur footpad together (fur

Step 12

Step 13

Step 14

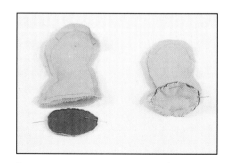

Step 15

Step 16

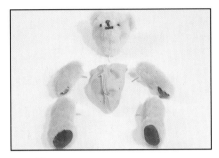

Step 17

Step 18

Step 19

inside) and sew. Fit the footpad into the leg with the felt to the inside. Make sure that point 5 on the footpad lines up with point 5 on the leg. It is safest to pin and baste before sewing (step 15).

Turn the arms and legs the right way out and stuff. Insert the joints, using the smaller discs this time. Make sure that arms and legs are perfectly matched. Sew up the arm and leg openings with blanket stitch. Cut the paw patches from dark brown felt and sew to the arms with buttonhole silk (step 16).

Now you have made the sections of the bear and all that remains is to assemble them (step 17).

Turn the body the right way out. Place the point of the cotter-pin sticking out of the head into the point where the seams meet at the top of the body. Place a large plastic disc on to the pin and curl the points under with pliers. NB: make sure you press the pins tightly together or the head will come loose in time (step 18).

Attach the arms and legs in the same way, using large discs for each of the body joints (step 19). Finally stuff the body. If you want the teddy to stand up straight make sure you compact the stuffing well in the lower half of the body. Sew up the back seam with blanket stitch. Prise out the fur from the seams with a needle.

Clothes

Dungarees are ideal for babies and for baby bears, too. In winter they can be worn with a waistcoat.

You will find the cutting patterns for the **dungarees** on pages 66/67. You will need a largish remnant of fine needlecord and two buttons.

Fold the fabric double and cut 2 trouser fronts with bib and 2 trouser backs without bib (adding 0.5 cm/$\frac{1}{4}$ in seam allowance). For the straps cut two strips of the required length. Sew up the side seams and inside the outside legs. Make a narrow hem at the top back and front. Fold the straps in half lengthways, turn in the edges and sew together. Sew the straps to the back of the trousers and make the buttonholes at the other end. Sew two buttons to the top of the bib.

You will find cutting patterns for the **waistcoat** on pages 68/69. You need a remnant of small-patterned cotton fabric and a small piece of fine needlecord. Fold the fabrics, place patterns along the fold and, with seam allowance, cut out once from the cotton and once from the needlecord. With the fabrics right side together sew the shoulder seams. Line the cord waistcoat with the cotton waistcoat, turn the right way out and then sew to close opening.

You will find the cutting pattern for the **trousers** on pages 68/69. You will need about 0.3 m/$\frac{1}{4}$ yd needlecord.

Fold the fabric. Cut out the trouser section twice (adding 0.5 cm/$\frac{1}{4}$ in seam allowance). For straps and cross-straps cut three strips of the required length. Sew up the leg seams. Hem the waist. The shoulder straps should be attached at the front, crossed at the back and fastened with press-studs. Sew the cross-strap behind the front of the shoulder straps.

Peter the Great

He is the star of the nursery. Peter is 1 m/3½ ft tall when fully grown. When making a large bear like this it's a good idea to include small pieces of left-over fur in the filling. Peter will look equally stunning if you make him into a dark brown, long-haired bear with light paws.

Making up

Cut all sections, except for the nose, with 1 cm/⅜ in seam allowance. From

Materials
1 m/1 yd light brown teddy fur
   (1.4 m/54 in wide)
0.2 m/¼ yd dark brown teddy fur
   (1.4 m/54 in wide)
2 glass eyes
about 1.5 kg/3¼ lb dacron and
   polyester filling

the dark fur cut the following pieces: inside ears (2), footpads (2), paw patches (2), nose (1). Cut all other sections from the light fur. (Check

sewing cotton
dark brown cotton
2 × 20 cm/7¾ in lengths brown
   twisted cord
scissors
dressmaker's chalk
The cutting patterns are on pages
   76/77.

which way the pile lies.) Copy all the pattern markings on to the fabric.

Sew in the darts on the body section and sew the back and front

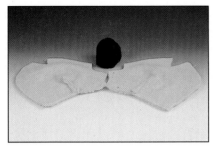

Step 1

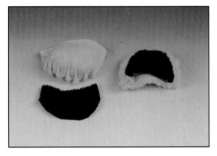

Step 2

Step 3

Step 4

together, leaving the neck open. Turn the body the right way out and stuff it with filling.

Sew in the darts on the side head sections and join the chin seam (step 1). Matching up the numbers, sew the centre head section between the two side sections, leaving openings at the muzzle, ears and neck. Sew the four sections of the muzzle together, matching up the markings. Sew the completed muzzle into place.

Next put in the darts in both outside ear sections. Place each outer ear right sides together with an inner ear and sew round the curved edge. Leave the straight edges open. Turn the ears the right way out and (with the head still the wrong side out) sew into the ear openings with the inside ear to the front (step 2).

Turn the head the right way out and sew to the body at the neck edge, leaving a small opening. Stuff the head and sew up the opening with blanket stitch.

Sew the darts in the four leg and two leg gusset sections. Place two leg sections together and pin the side seam, leaving the curved edge at the top open. Place the leg gusset in the opening. Sew all the side seams except for a small opening for turning, but leave the bottom open for the footpad. Sew in the footpads, matching up the markings. Turn the legs the right way out and stuff (step 3).

Sew the dark paw patches to the insides of the arms and sew the inside and outside arm sections together, leaving an opening for turning. Turn the arms the right way out and stuff them.

Make a knot in the end of one of the twisted cords and pass it from the inside through the point marked 'X' on the inner arm. Then sew up the arm opening with blanket stitch. The cord then goes into the body at the 'X' on the arm socket and out again on the opposite side (step 4). Thread the cord

through the 'X' on the other arm and knot it. Sew up the opening on this arm. Repeat with the other cord for the legs.

Fold the nose section along the dotted line into a large triangle and sew it with overcast stitches to the muzzle. Embroider the mouth and attach the eyes. You may find the method for inserting eyes detailed on page 34 the easiest to follow.

For the trousers you will need:

Materials
0.6 m/$\frac{5}{8}$ yd brown cotton (1.4 m/ 54 in wide)
0.5 m/$\frac{1}{2}$ yd red bias binding
red felt, 2 press-studs
6 decorative buttons
elastic
iron-on adhesive
The cutting patterns are on pages 68/69.

From the cotton cut the trousers front and back, the straps and cross-strap, allowing 1 cm/$\frac{3}{8}$ in seam allowance. Cut the trouser flap without seam allowance. From the red felt cut the pocket flaps and the decoration for the cross-strap without seam allowance. Sew up the inside and outside leg seams. Hem the waist and put in elastic. Turn up the trouser legs about 3 cm/$1\frac{1}{4}$ in on the right side and trim with bias binding. Trim the trouser flap with bias binding and fasten to the trouser front with 4 buttons. Fold the straps and cross-strap lengthways, turn the edges in and sew. Sew red bias binding to the straps. Attach the straps with buttons to the front of the trousers, cross them behind and fasten with press-studs. Sew the cross strap into place behind the front shoulder straps. Iron the pocket flaps to the trouser fronts and the decoration to the cross-strap.

Panda

It may be extremely rare for a panda family in a zoo to produce a cub, but it's not a problem for the teddy-lover. In a couple of hours he can create a lovable black and white baby panda with an appealing, sad face. And why not make a mother for the baby panda, too?

Materials
0.35 m/⅜ yd white fur fabric
   (1.4 m/54 in wide)
0.25 m/¼ yd black fur fabric
   (1.4 m/54 in wide)
dacron and polyester filling
remnant black imitation leather
2 black button eyes
1 upholstery needle
scissors, pins, dressmaker's chalk
The cutting patterns are on pages 78/79
The big bear measures 40 cm/15¾ in
The baby measures 30 cm/11¾ in

Making up
Cut out the pattern sections adding 1 cm/⅜ in seam allowance, checking which way the pile lies and remembering to copy all the markings on the patterns on to the fabric.

Place the outside leg sections right sides together with the inside leg sections and pin the long front and back edges together, placing the pins at right angles to the edge and pushing the fur inside. Sew the seams. Place the footpads in the bottom of the legs, matching up the numbers. Turn the legs the right way out. Sew the outside and inside arm sections together along the outside edge and turn the arms the right way out.

To make the head, place the ear sections right sides together and sew round the curved edge. Turn the ears and sew in the correct position (number 10) on the back head section. Fold the front head section on to the back head section with right sides together (ears inside) and sew along the top of the head, catching the ears in the seam.

On the right side, neatly sew the black eye patches to the front of the head. Then place the two head sections right sides together and sew up the back and front centre seams. On the muzzle, start by sewing up the centre side and then the side seams. Sew the muzzle into the round opening at the front of the head and sew the dart on the neck edge.

Sew the centre back and centre front seams. Finally sew the side, inside leg and shoulder seams. Join the arms and legs at the appropriate openings in the body and turn the body the right way out. Stuff the legs, body, arms and head with dacron and polyester filling. Gather up the neck edge on the head and body to roughly 30 cm/11¾ in circumference. Sew the head by hand to the body using strong thread.

Place the tail sections right sides together, sew and turn right side out. Stuff the tail with a little filling and sew to the body along the marked line. From the imitation leather cut a circle about 5 cm/2 in. in diameter for the nose. Make a row of running stitches 0.5 cm/¼ in from the edge and gather up to shape the nose. Knot the ends of the thread and stuff the nose with a little filling. Sew the nose to the centre of the muzzle. Finally sew the eyes to the black eye patches.

Patterns

Mother bear's dress

(red)

Front 1 × along fold
back 2 ×
front yoke 1 × along fold
back yoke 2 ×

Dungarees

(blue)

Teddy bear gang – smaller bear
dungarees 4 ×
two straps, each 2 × 18 cm/$\frac{3}{4}$ × 7 in

Teddy bear gang – larger bear
dungarees 4 ×
two straps, each 2.8 × 25 cm/1 × 9$\frac{3}{4}$ in

Bear family – smaller bear
dungarees 4 ×
four straps 2 × 5 cm/$\frac{3}{4}$ × 2 in

Father bear's jacket

(black)

back 1 ×
revers 2 ×
front 2 ×
sleeve 2 ×
collar 2 ×

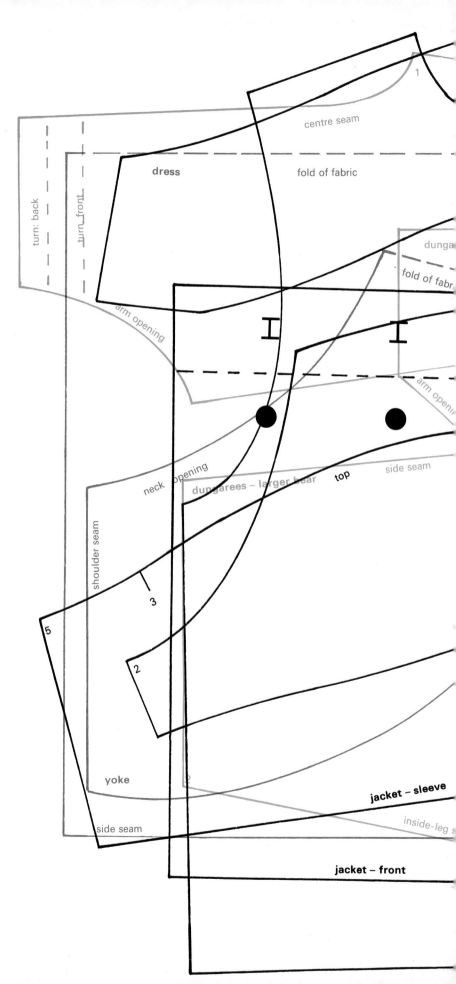

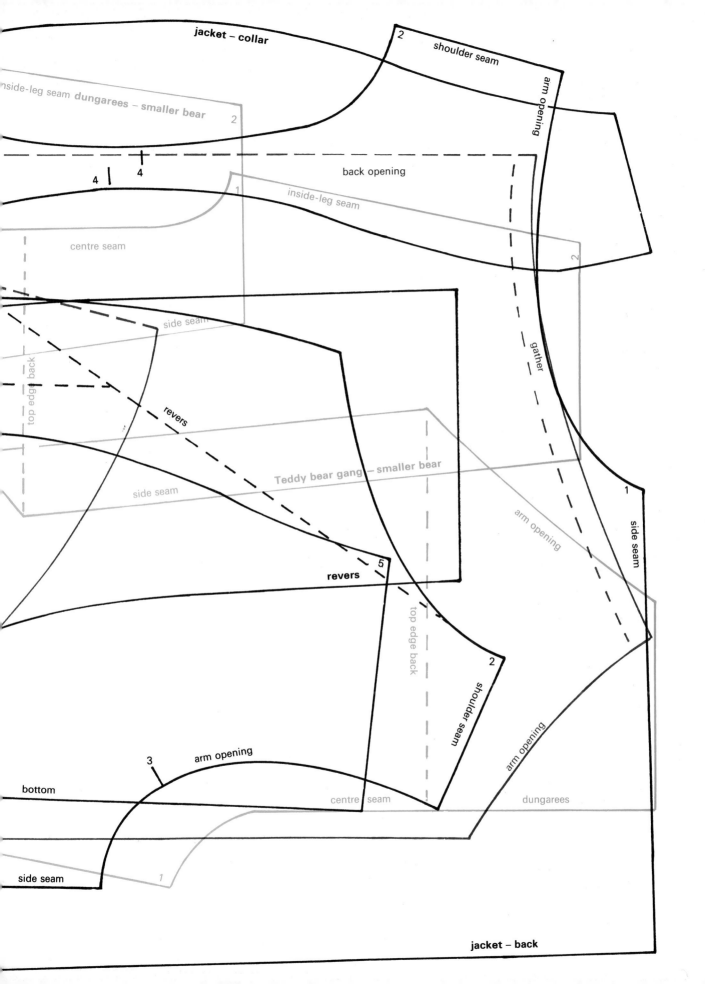

Peter the Great's trousers

(black)

trouser A and B 2 ×
trouser back A and B 2 ×
pocket flaps 2 ×
straps 2 ×, extend length
   to 57 cm/22¼ in
cross-strap 1 ×
trouser flap 1 ×
cross-strap ornament 2 ×

Bill and Ben's bib

(blue)

bib 1 ×

Teddy bear gang waistcoat

small waistcoat (blue)
2 × along fold

large waistcoat (red)
2 × along fold

Teddy bear gang trousers

large trousers (red) 2 ×
straps, each 2.8 × 25 cm/1 × 9¾ in
cross-strap 2.8 × 7 cm/1 × 2¾ in

small trousers (red) 2 ×
straps, each 2 × 18 cm/¾ × 7 in
cross-strap 2 × 5 cm/¾ × 2 in

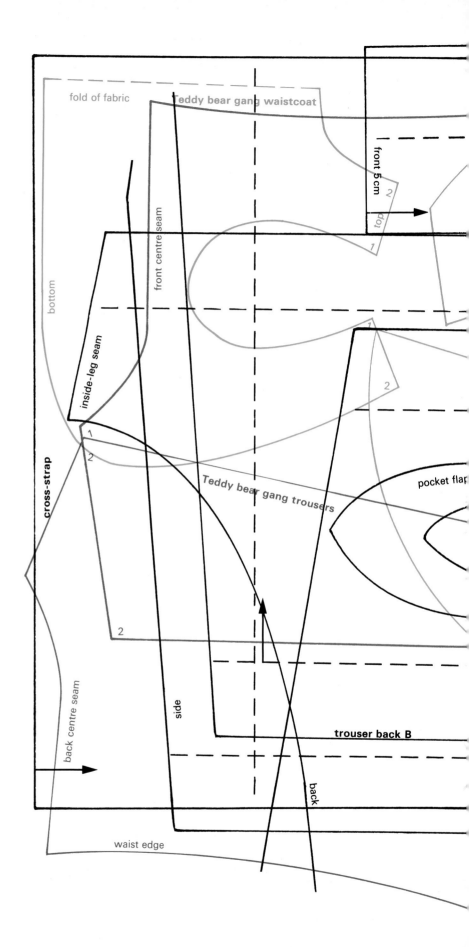

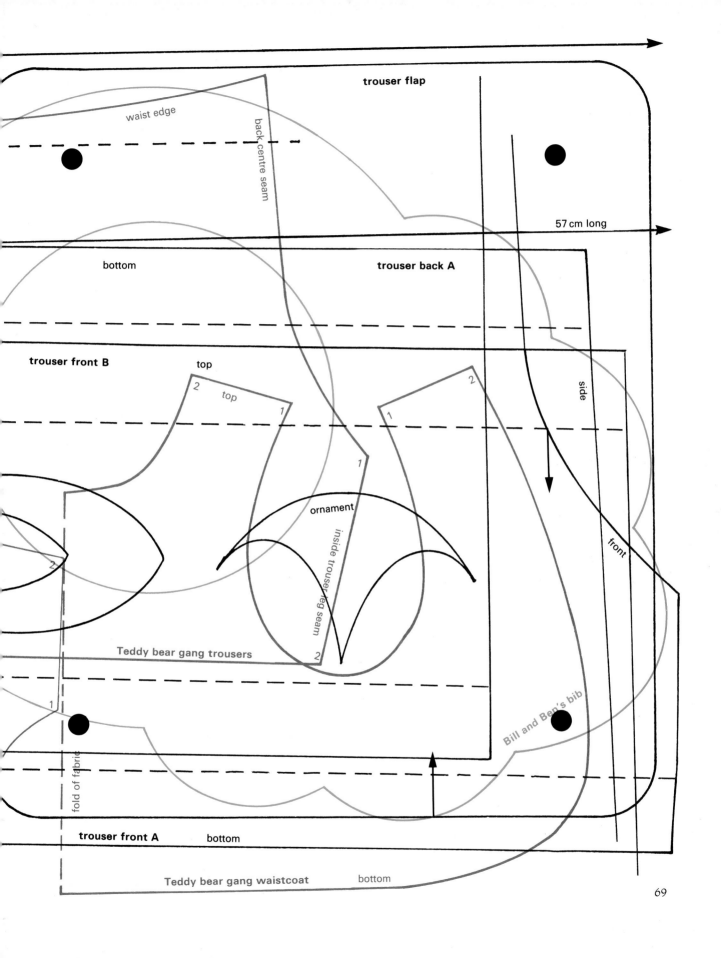

trouser flap

waist edge

back centre seam

57 cm long

bottom

trouser back A

trouser front B

top

2 top

top 1

2

1

1

side

ornament

inside trouser leg seam

front

2

2

Teddy bear gang trousers

1

Bill and Ben's bib

fold of fabric

trouser front A   bottom

Teddy bear gang waistcoat   bottom

69

Bill and Ben

(blue and black)

front head 2 ×
back head 2 ×
arm 2 ×
tummy 2 ×
back 2 ×
leg 2 ×
ear 2 × in dark fabric,
ear 2 × in light fabric
footpad 2 × in dark fabric
paw 2 × in dark fabric
tongue 1 ×
muzzle 1 ×
front centre head 1 ×

Quick and easy bear

(red)

body 2 ×
paws, each 1 ×

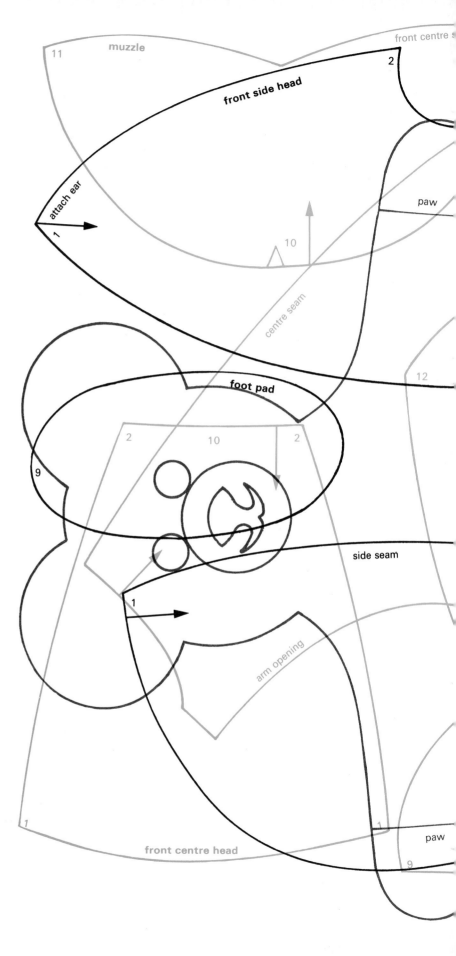

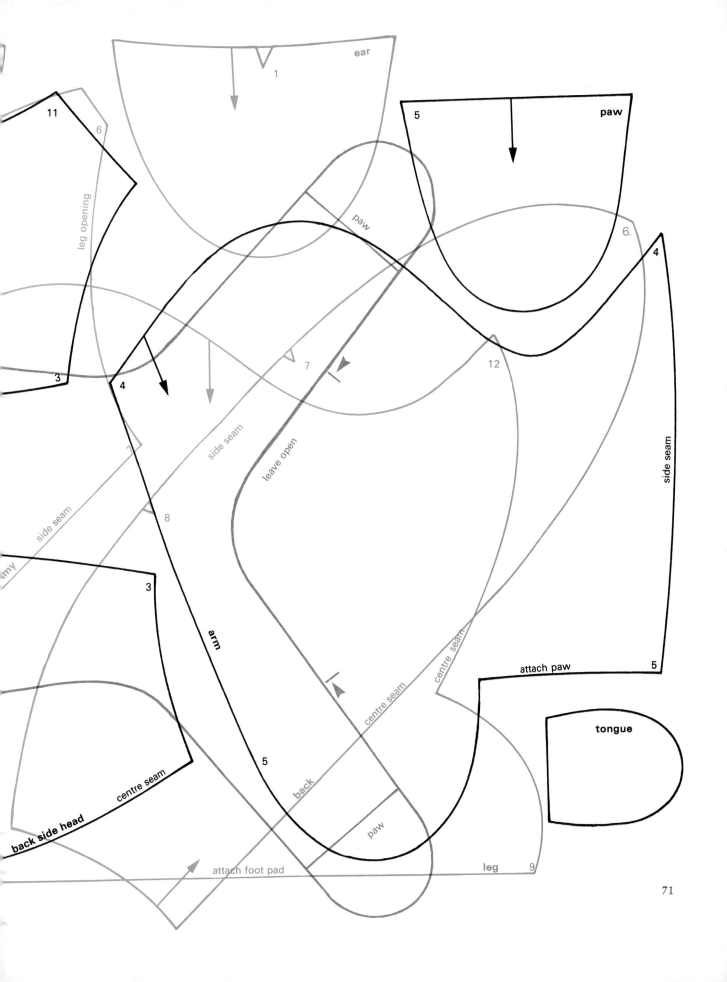

ear

1

paw

5

11

6

6.

4

leg opening

3

4

paw

7

12

side seam

side seam

leave open

7

side seam

8

3

arm

side seam

centre seam

attach paw

5

5

tongue

centre seam

back side head

centre seam

5

back

paw

attach foot pad

leg

9

71

Bear family

Mother and father
centre head (black) 1 ×
ear (black) 4 ×
inside arm (black) 2 ×
outside arm (black) 2 ×
footpad (black) 2 ×
muzzle (blue) 1 ×
side head (blue) 2 ×
back (blue) 2 ×
tummy (red) 2 ×
outside leg (red) 2 ×
inside leg (red) 2 ×

For the bear offspring, turn to pages 74/75

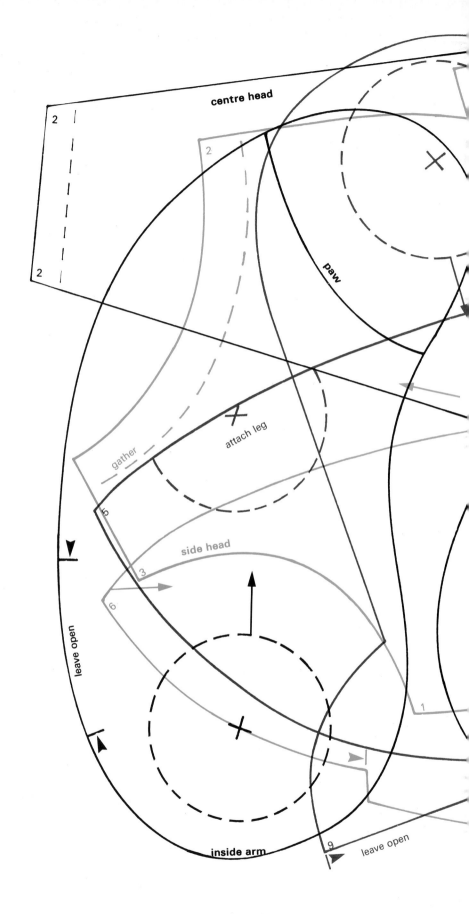

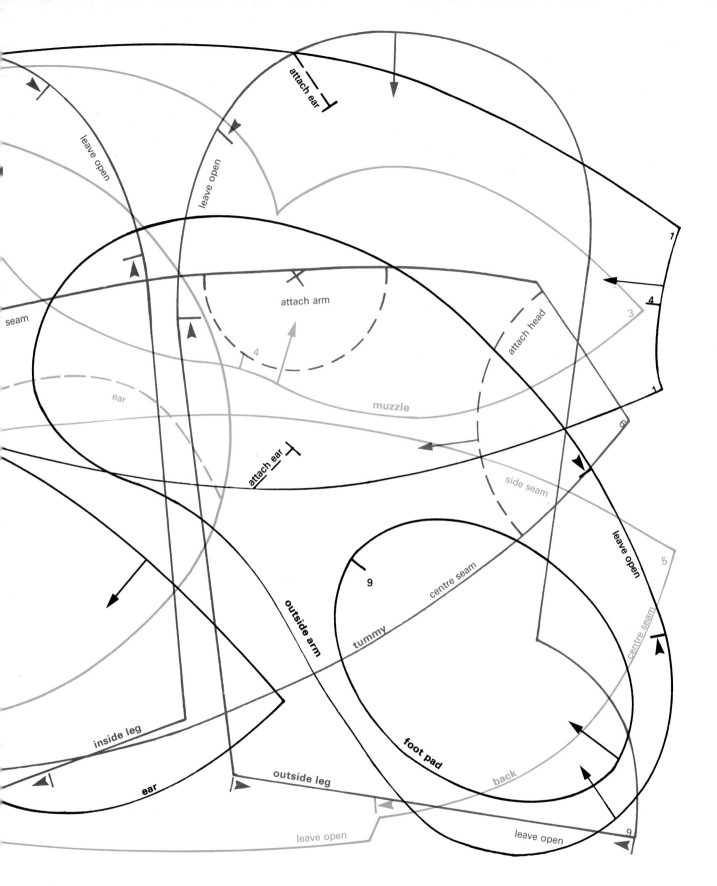

leave open

leave open

attach ear

leave open

seam

attach arm

attach head

4

3

4

1

1

6

ear

muzzle

attach ear

side seam

leave open

5

9

centre seam

centre seam

outside arm

tummy

inside leg

foot pad

back

ear

outside leg

9

leave open

leave open

73

Teddy bear gang

(black)

side body 2 ×
side head 2 ×
ear, each 2 ×
leg, each 2 ×
arm, each 2 ×
footpad 2 ×
centre head 1 ×

The patterns in red are
for the small bears.

Bear family

The patterns in blue are
for the small bear in the
bear family.

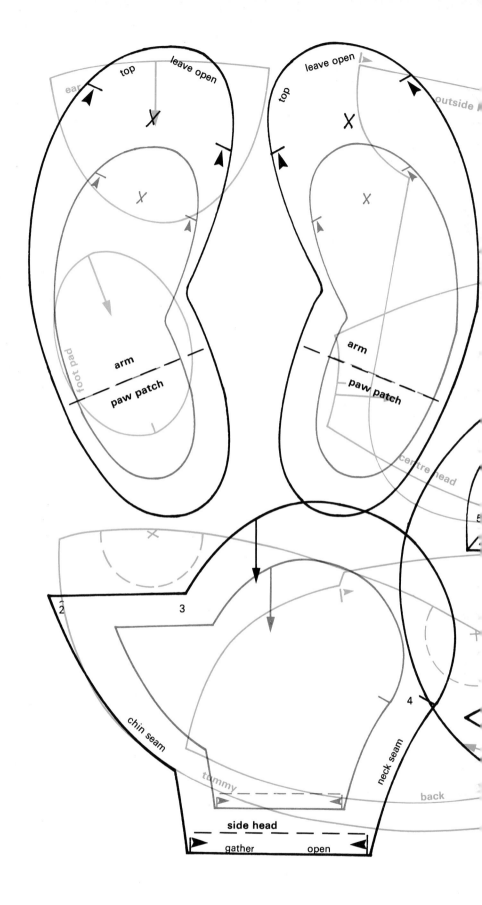

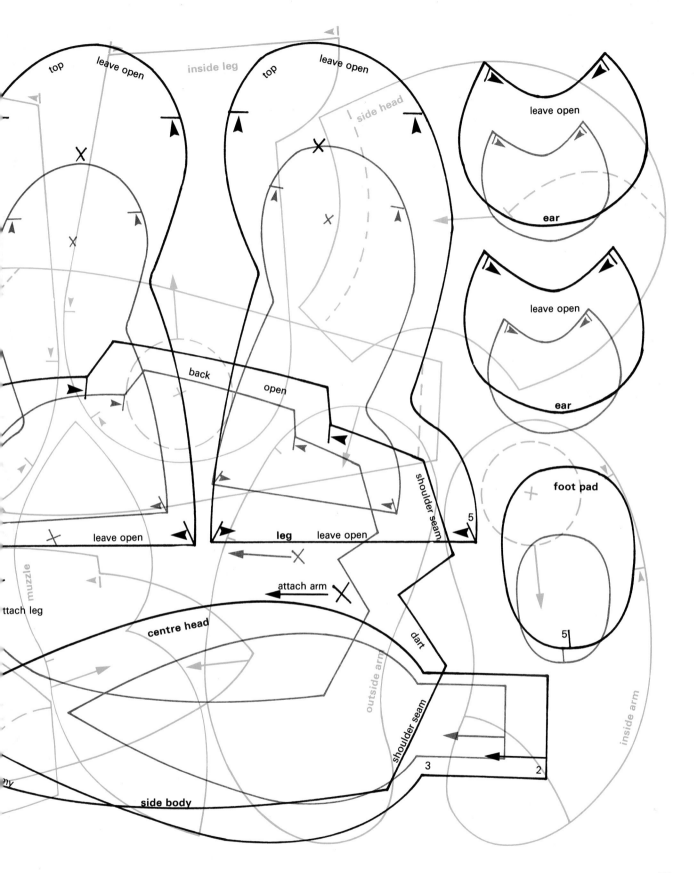

top

leave open

inside leg

top

leave open

side head

leave open

ear

leave open

ear

back

open

side head

muzzle

shoulder seam

5

foot pad

attach leg

centre head

leave open

leg

leave open

attach arm

dart

outside arm

inside arm

5

shoulder seam

side body

3

2

tummy

Peter the great

arm (black) 4 ×
muzzle (black) 4 ×
inside ear (black) 2 ×
footpad (black) 2 ×
nose (black) 1 ×
outside ear (black) 2 ×
centre leg (blue) 2 ×
centre head A and B (blue) 4 ×
leg A and B (blue) 4 ×
side head (red) 2 ×
tummy A and B (orange) 2 ×
back A and B (orange) 2 ×

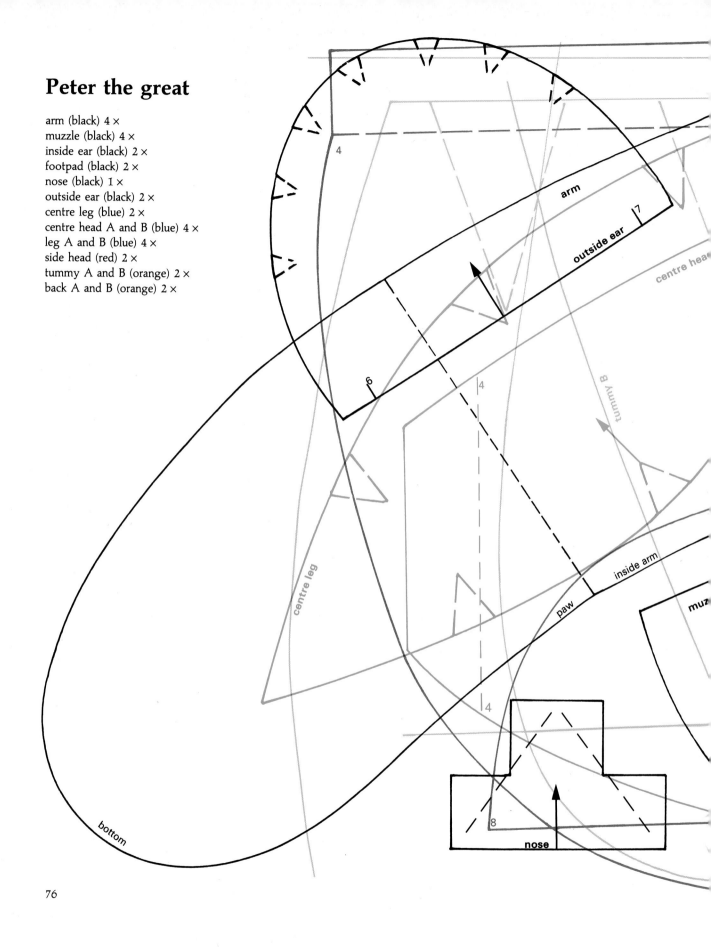

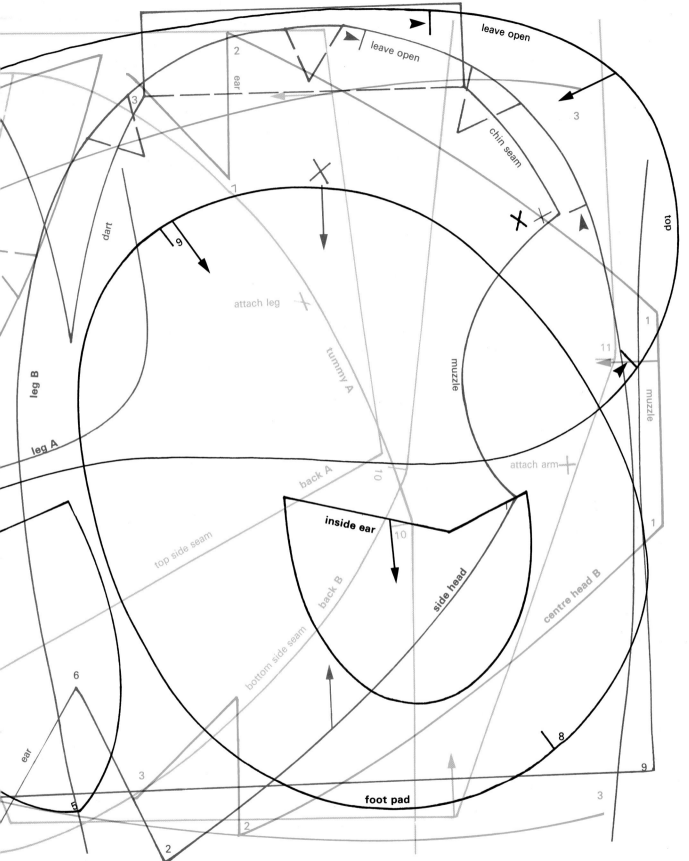

leave open

leave open

top

chin seam

ear

2

3

3

1

11

muzzle

muzzle

dart

9

leg B

attach leg

tummy A

leg A

attach arm

7

back A

10

inside ear

10

side head

centre head B

top side seam

back B

bottom side seam

6

ear

8

9

3

3

2

5

foot pad

2

Polar bear

(black)

outside body 2 ×
inside body 2 ×
muzzle 1 ×
head gusset 1 ×
tail 1 ×
footpad 4 ×
ear 4 ×

Panda

(large)

All red pattern sections are cut from
black fur fabric.

outside arm 2 ×
inside arm 2 ×
outside leg 2 ×
inside leg 2 ×
footpad 2 ×
eye patch 2 ×
tail 2 ×
ear 4 ×

All blue pattern sections are cut
from white fur fabric.

back 2 ×
front and back head 2 ×
tummy 2 ×
muzzle 1 ×

All orange pattern sections are for
the small panda.

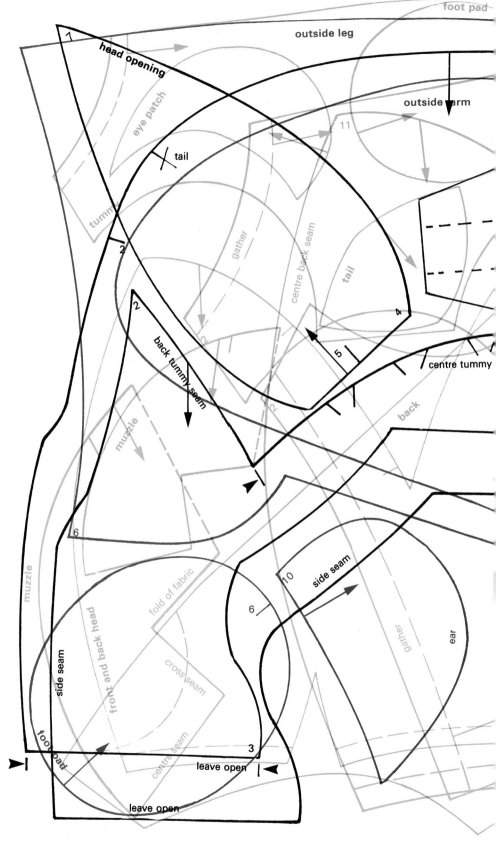

outside body

tummy

ear 4 4

back seam 7

9

1 1

ear pleat

9

attach ear

10

inside body

7

1

12

5

8

eye patch

back

13

3

leave open

leave open

11

centre seam

outside leg

tail

ear

front centre seam

seam

3

4

eye

4

inside leg

inside arm

outside arm

13

neck seam

1 1

muzzle

3

inside arm

side seam

attach tail

5

centre seam

13

14

3

front and back head

gather

centre seam

6

foot pad

inside leg

Acknowledgments
Photographs Harald Nadolny, Herne;
Margarete Steiff GmbH, Giengen
Diagrams Harald Nadolny, Herne

First published 1989 by The Hamlyn
Publishing Group Limited, a division of
the Octopus Publishing Group,
Michelin House, 81 Fulham Road,
London SW3 6RB

First impression 1989

Published in the U.S.A. by
Stackpole Books
Cameron and Kelker Sts.
Harrisburg, PA 17105

Reprinted 1989

Several generations of bears meet

The instructions given in this book
have been carefully checked by the
authors and the copyright holder but
they are not guaranteed correct. The
authors, the copyright holder and the
publisher accept no liability for any
damage, personal, material, financial or
otherwise that may occur.

Typeset by Servis Filmsetting
Limited, Manchester M13 0LU

Printed by Mandarin Offset,
Hong Kong

Library of Congress Card Number 89-21813